How to Win a Fight with a Conservative

by Daniel Kurtzman

SOURCEBOOKS HYSTERIA™
AN IMPRINT OF SOURCEBOOKS, INC.®
NAPERVILLE, ILLINOIS

Published by Sourcebooks Hysteria, an imprint of Sourcebooks Inc.
P.O. Box 4410, Naperville, Illinois 60567-4410
(630) 961-3900
Fax: (630) 961-2168
www.sourcebooks.com

Printed and bound in Canada
WC   10   9   8   7   6

Dedication

FOR MY WIFE,

LAURA,

AND

FOR MY PARENTS,

KEN AND CARYL,

AND MY BROTHER, TODD

Table of Contents

Introduction

Have you ever been so infuriated by a political argument that you've been tempted to invite your opponent to go hunting and "accidentally" shoot him in the face?

Do you ever engage in heated debates with obnoxious conservative wingnuts, only to find yourself sputtering and stuttering, unable to articulate your beliefs?

How many times have you listened to the delusional rantings of an insufferable colleague, loudmouthed uncle, or neighborhood blowhard while fantasizing about delivering the verbal smackdown they so richly deserve?

We've all been there—butting heads with some

half-wit who refuses to submit to the inevitable wisdom of our political views. Whether you're a liberal, progressive, Democrat, independent, or someone who's just tired of conservatives and their bullshit, chances are that at some point you've walked away (perhaps under the supervision of men in white coats) from a political argument seething with rage, indignation, frustration, or resentment.

Such is the sorry state of political discourse in 21st-century America. For too long, partisan Americans have had to settle for antiquated and inefficient methods of resolving their differences (incoherent rage, *O'Reilly Factor* appearances, pistol duels). But it doesn't have to be this way. With a shrewd and sensible approach, you can learn to make political arguments that actually work. This book offers a roadmap to success that will help you size up, knock down, and win over your conservative rivals—without making yourself the target of the local militia, a Pat Robertson fatwa, or a Swift Boat–style smear campaign.

With the help of some basic, common-sense rules of engagement, we'll provide you with a solid foundation from which to launch your campaigns of political reeducation. We will show you how to:

★ Understand what drives your adversaries and their nutty ideas
★ Avoid deadly pitfalls that would otherwise sink your own best arguments
★ Learn how to win friends while antagonizing people
★ Identify bullshitters in their various guises
★ Slice through Swiss cheese logic and expose fallacious reasoning
★ Make kick-ass arguments on a range of hot-button issues
★ Bludgeon your enemy with devastating sound bites, witty rejoinders, and damning facts
★ Hurl imaginative insults by selecting from 27,000 possibilities, should all else fail

No matter what predicament you may find yourself in, this book contains indispensable tips and strategies to match your motivations. If you're hoping to rally potential recruits to a political cause, save a loved one's soul, or impress a girl, we'll show you how to maximize your chances for success. If you're looking to humiliate a pompous windbag, expose a shameless liar, or deflect an insurgent attack, we'll show you how to respond with overwhelming force.

Will you be able to win over every misguided right-wing hack? Let's be honest. Some conservatives are so unteachably ignorant, so self-righteously closed-minded, there is literally nothing you can say—or no legal torture method you can employ—to enlighten them. If you're planning to mix it up with conservatives who fit that profile, you'll need a blunter instrument than this book with which to beat them over the head.

Fortunately, there are plenty of conservatives out there who are rational people, have a passing acquaintance with fact-based reasoning, or, failing that, are at least taking the right medication to control their condition. By following the strategies outlined here, you stand every chance of beating these types of conservatives in a war of words. Or even if you can't beat them, you can jackhammer a few winning points into their brains that will send them into a tizzy of cognitive dissonance and wreck havoc on their reality.

Politics was never meant to be a spectator sport. Political debate is simply too important to be left to the so-called experts in Washington and the media, who invariably just screw it up for the rest of us. That's why it falls on ordinary citizens like you—whether you're an unpracticed neophyte or battle-scarred politico—to take matters into your own hands. If conservatism is to be defeated, the battle must be fought hand-to-hand and street-to-street. It must be fought wherever the enemy lurks—whether in the next cubicle, across the Thanksgiving dinner table, at NASCAR races, church socials, or Halliburton shareholder meetings.

It's up to you, gentle reader, to take the fight to conservatives and defend America against every intolerant, corrupt, puritanical, greed-mongering, war-agitating, Constitution-trampling ideal for which they stand.

If you don't, the wingnuts will have won.

★ **CHAPTER 1** ★

What It Means to Be a Liberal

Somebody came along and said 'liberal' means 'soft on crime, soft on drugs, soft on Communism, soft on defense, and we're gonna tax you back to the Stone Age because people shouldn't have to go to work if they don't want to.' And instead of saying, 'Well, excuse me, you right-wing, reactionary, xeno-phobic, homophobic, anti-education, anti-choice, pro-gun, Leave-It-to-Beaver trip back to the '50s,' we cowered in the corner and said, 'Please don't hurt me.'

—NBC's *The West Wing*

No one can pinpoint the exact moment it happened, but sometime in the last quarter century, between Ronald Reagan's withering ridicule of all things liberal and George W. Bush's bullying crusade to stamp out political dissent, conservatives gave liberalism a giant wedgie.

Liberalism didn't see it coming. It was busy navel-gazing and admiring itself in the mirror when conservatives snuck up from behind, grabbed it by its tighty-whities, and hung it up on the flagpole, where it kicked and flailed as conservatives pointed and taunted and called it a pantywaist and a loser.

Democrats, even some Republicans, used to wear the liberal label with pride. Time was, liberalism was a word that conjured such core American principles as social justice, national compassion, and human freedom. But then conservatives had an idea. What if liberalism could be turned into an embarrassing perversion, like pedophilia, or a disease, like leprosy? And so they told anyone who would listen that liberals were sick, weak, deranged, traitorous perverts.

The problem is, liberals stood there and took the abuse. They let conservatives bullyrag them, beat them down, and get inside their heads until they ran away with their hands over their ears, screaming, "I'm not a liberal!" And thus a proud ideology was thrown under the bus.

Sure, recent Democratic victories may have given liberals reason to rejoice. But the pattern of victimization continues, with liberals still letting conservatives keep them on the defensive. Enough. If liberals hope to be persuasive and start kicking some serious conservative ass, they need to stand tall, fight back, and confidently declare who they are and what they stand for.

That's why, as a first step in girding for battle with conservatives, it's essential to have a firm fix on your own beliefs. Take the following quiz to determine where you fit in the larger liberal mix.

What Breed of Liberal Are You?

Choose the answers that most closely match your ideological leanings.

1. Which bumper sticker would you most likely put on your car?

_____A. I'm Already Against the *Next* War

_____B. Nice Hummer—Sorry About Your Penis

_____C. America: One Nation Under Surveillance

_____D. Of Course It Hurts, You're Getting Screwed by an Elephant

_____E. Evolution Is Just a Theory . . .Kind of Like Gravity

_____F. May the Fetus You Save Be Gay

2. A second civil war has just broken out in America. Who is to blame?

_____A. Imperialistic neocons—for launching simultaneous wars against Iran, North Korea, and France

_____B. Global warming deniers—for bringing us an eco-apocalypse

_____C. The South—for never having gotten over the fact that they lost the first War of Northern Aggression

_____D. Corporate greedmongers—for outsourcing every last American job to Bangalore

_____E. FOX News—for fomenting a war with a flashy "March to Civil War" logo and theme music

_____F. Bible-thumping puritans—for banning abortion, gay people, and sex

3. An asteroid is headed for Earth. You have a seat on the last shuttle off the planet. If you could bring only one book with which to build a future civilization, what would it be?

_____A. *Zen and the Art of Motorcycle Maintenance,* by Robert Pirsig

_____B. *An Inconvenient Truth,* by Al Gore

_____C. *The Hitchhiker's Guide to the Galaxy,* by Douglas Adams

_____D. *A People's History of the United States,* by Howard Zinn

_____E. *Origin of Species,* by Charles Darwin

_____F. *America (The Book): A Citizen's Guide to Democracy Inaction,* by Jon Stewart

4. If the Founding Fathers were alive today, they would be most appalled by which of the following?

_____A. The Republicans' blatant manipulation of terror fears for partisan gain

_____B. America's crack-like addiction to Saudi oil

_____C. President Bush's blatant dictatorial power grab

_____D. Government of, by, and for corporate cronies

_____E. The hijacking of government by radical Christian wackjobs

_____F. That hemp is illegal. Come on, what wasn't clear about the "pursuit of happiness"?

5. If you could time-travel back to any historical event and bring one thing with you, what would you choose?

_____A. The 1967 Summer of Love—with a truckload of condoms

_____B. The dawn of the Industrial Revolution—with a copy of the Kyoto Protocol

_____C. The day before Hurricane Katrina hit New Orleans—with FEMA

_____D. The day Monica Lewinsky brought Bill Clinton pizza—with a copy of the Starr Report

_____E. Election Day 2000 in Palm Beach County—with non-butterfly ballots

_____F. The night of Howard Dean's 2004 Iowa concession speech—with a tranquilizer dart

6. If you were a candidate for political office, what would your theme song be?

_____A. "Peace Train," by Cat Stevens

_____B. "It's Not Easy Being Green," by Kermit the Frog

_____C. "Fight the Power," by Public Enemy

_____D. "Born in the U.S.A.," by Bruce Springsteen

_____E. "I Still Haven't Found What I'm Looking For," by U2

_____F. "Not Ready to Make Nice," by the Dixie Chicks

7. If you could pile any three people into a naked pyramid, who would you choose?

_____A. George W. Bush, Dick Cheney, and Donald Rumsfeld

_____B. The CEOs of Exxon, Chevron, and Shell

_____C. Antonin Scalia, Clarence Thomas, and Samuel Alito

_____D. Enron's Jeffrey Skilling, Andrew Fastow, and the ghost of Ken Lay

_____E. Bill O'Reilly, Ann Coulter, and Rush Limbaugh

_____F. Revs. Pat Robertson, Jerry Falwell, and Ted Haggard

Scoring

If you answered mostly As, you're a _Peace Patroller_, also known as an antiwar liberal. You believe in stopping American imperial conquest and supporting our troops by bringing them home.

If you answered mostly Bs, you're an _Eco-Avenger_, also known as an environmentalist or tree hugger. You believe in saving the planet from the clutches of air-fouling, oil-drilling, earth-raping conservative fossil fools.

If you answered mostly Cs, you're a _Social Justice Crusader_, also known as a rights activist. You believe in equality, fairness, and preventing neo-Confederate conservative troglodytes from rolling back fifty years of civil rights gains.

If you answered mostly Ds, you're a *Working Class Warrior*. You believe that the little guy is getting screwed by conservative greedmongers and corporate criminals, and you're not going to take it anymore.

If you answered mostly Es, you're a *Reality-Based Intellectualist*, also known as the liberal elite. You are a proud member of what's known as the reality-based community, where science, reason, and non-Jesus-based thought reign supreme.

If you answered mostly Fs, you're a *New Left Hipster*, also known as a MoveOn.org liberal, a Netroots activist, or a *Daily Show* fanatic. You believe in all of the above, plus the fact that virtually nothing conservatives say can be believed.

If your answers don't match any of the above, that means you're a label-defying iconoclast or a hybrid of various types. Consider it a point of pride.

If you don't stand for anything, you don't stand for anything!

—George W. Bush

As you can see, liberals are a diverse breed. But at bottom, there is a core set of beliefs and a common cause that unites them all. With that in mind, we present . . .

THE LIBERAL MANIFESTO

Liberals believe in clean air, diplomacy, stem cells, living wages, body armor for our troops, government accountability, and that exercising the right to dissent is the highest form of patriotism.

Liberals believe in reading actual books, going to war as a last resort, separating church and hate, and doing what Jesus would actually do, instead of lobbying for upper-class tax cuts and fantasizing about the apocalypse.

Liberals believe in civil rights, the right to privacy, and that evolution and global warming aren't just theories but incontrovertible scientific facts.

Liberals believe there ought to be a constitutional amendment that (1) prohibits another Bush from ever occupying the White House, and (2) prevents George W. Bush from ever becoming baseball commissioner before he does to our national pastime what he did for America.

Liberals believe in rescuing people from flooded streets and rooftops, even if they're too poor to vote Republican.

Liberals believe that supporting our troops means treating our wounded vets like the heroes they are, and not leaving them to languish in rat-infested military hospitals under the outsourced management of incompetent cronies who think they're running a Taco Bell franchise.

Liberals believe in pheromones, sex ed, solar panels, voting paper trails, the common good, and that, no matter how fascinating a story it may be, a president should never sit around in a state of total paralysis reading "My Pet Goat" while America is under attack.

And above all, liberals believe that it's time to come together as a country and put a collective boot in the ass of shameless conservative fearmongers, hate merchants, and scapegoaters who are sucking the freedom out of all our souls.

Rate Your Partisan Intensity Quotient (PIQ)

Beyond basic ideology, we also need to assess your partisan temperament. Are you the type of person who eagerly engages conservatives in debate or do you avoid confrontation at all costs? Answer the following questions, and we'll rate your PIQ.

1. Your neighbor has just placed a very large 2008 Giuliani sign on her lawn. Do you:

_____A. Show respect for her right to free speech?

_____B. Put up an even larger Hillary 2008 sign?

_____C. Take down her sign in the middle of the night?

_____D. Graffiti your own Hillary sign and then publicly accuse her of defacing your property?

2. You're at an antiwar rally. A Republican heckler appears out of nowhere and begins chanting "USA! USA!" while hoisting a sign printed with "Kick Their Ass and Take Their Gas!" Do you:

_____A. Embrace him in the spirit of tolerance and respect for diversity?

_____B. Move to another part of the crowd to avoid a confrontation?

_____C. Hoist up your own sign and drown him out with your own chant?

_____D. Wrestle him to the ground and smack him repeatedly with your "Think Peace" sign?

3. You're in the voting booth attempting to cast your ballot for the Democratic candidate, but no matter what button you touch on the Diebold machine, the Republican candidate's name keeps coming up. Do you:

_____A. Cast your vote anyway? (How much does one vote really matter?)

_____B. Alert a poll worker to the problem?

_____C. Alert the DNC and the media to the problem?

_____D. Consult your Internet printout, "How to Hack a Diebold Machine in Under Five Minutes," and change your vote to the Democrat? Repeat as necessary.

4. You've just been given the opportunity to meet President Bush and have a brief face-to-face encounter. Would you:

_____A. Tell him what an honor it is to meet him?

_____B. Think about what a schmuck he is but hold your tongue out of respect?

_____C. Grill him on his exit strategy for Iraq?

_____D. Tell him you preferred him when he was a drunken AWOL cokehead?

Scoring your PIQ

Award yourself zero points for every A, one point for every B, two points for every C, and three points for every D.

11-12: Severe ★★★★★★★★★★★★

You're a *Flame-Throwing Revolutionary*. You may be one wiretapped phone call away from Gitmo.

8-10: High ★★★★★★★★★★

You're a *Fierce Fighter*. You will argue politics any time and any place, even when it's not the topic at hand.

5-7: Elevated ★★★★★★★

You're a *Passionate Foot Soldier*. You readily engage in political debate but are apt to bail out before things get too testy.

2-4: Guarded ★★★★

You're a *Polite Observer*. You partake in the occasional political discussion but generally get more satisfaction out of arguing about *American Idol* than you do arguing politics.

0-1: Low ★

You're a *Noncombatant*. You're liable to wave the white flag and run for the hills at the slightest sign of political discord. Time to grow a pair.

WHAT'S YOUR STATE OF EMBATTLEMENT?

Everyone is familiar with the much-ballyhooed red vs. blue divide, which neatly separates America into Republican and Democratic states. But that obviously doesn't tell the whole story, as no state is uniformly red or blue. You've heard of other regional divides like the Bible Belt and the Rust Belt, but there are many other "belts" that describe partisan America. To determine your State of Embattlement, locate the belt below that most closely corresponds to your specific locality.

THE BELTS OF RED AMERICA
If you are a liberal living in . . .

The Chastity Belt (southern and middle America, where abstinence is all the rage)

The Saved Belt (God-fearing, churchgoing middle America)

The Dow Jones Belt (financial centers from New York to Chicago to Houston)

The Locked-and-Loaded Belt (gun country)

The Caviar and Cocaine Belt (home to the old money, country-club set)

The Border Belt (where 700-mile fences magically secure 2,000-mile borders)

. . .you are *Desperately Besieged*. You're surrounded by so many conservatives, it's like being the last person left at the end of a zombie movie. Arguing with them seems like a lost cause, and the best you can do is lay low and hide, lest they suck out your brain and turn you into one of them.

THE BELTS OF PURPLE AMERICA

If you are a liberal living in . . .

The Slot Jockey Belt (casino country, e.g., Nevada, Atlantic City, Mississippi River Valley)

The Stroke Belt (retirement communities in Florida)

The Kitsch Belt (small towns built around roadside kitsch and tourist schlock)

The Can't-Buckle-My-Belt (where the hefty portions match the people)

The Cookie-Cutter Belt (middle-class planned communities resembling *Desperate Housewives*'s Wisteria Lane)

The Bud Belt (where canned, flavor-free beer will always be king)

. . . you are *Battle-Hardened*. You have so many fights you want to pick with the conservatives all around you that you may not even know where to start.

THE BELTS OF BLUE AMERICA

If you are a liberal living in . . .

The Brokeback Belt (gay havens across America)

The Bagel Belt (urban areas with a high concentration of wisecracking Jews)

The Botox Belt (the land of the rich and plastic, from Manhattan to Hollywood)

The Ivory Tower Belt (enclaves dominated by intellectual and academic elites)

The Tofurky Belt (the land of militant vegans and naked tree-huggers)

The Bong Belt (stoner country, e.g., the core demographic of *The Daily Show* and *Real Time with Bill Maher*)

. . . you are *Safely Entrenched*. You're surrounded by so many people who agree with you that your arguing skills may have gone flabby from disuse.

Whatever situation you find yourself in, your goal is the same: Engage your enemies wherever they lurk. But first you must understand your enemy. . .

★ CHAPTER 2 ★

Know Your Enemy

If you know the enemy and know yourself, you need not fear the result of a hundred battles. If you know yourself but not the enemy, for every victory gained you will also suffer a defeat.

—Sun Tzu, *The Art of War*

B efore you engage conservatives in combat, it's important to have a clear understanding of exactly who your enemies are, including their core beliefs, specific ideological profile, and vision for America. Doing so will enable you to better dissect, ridicule, and exploit their weaknesses for maximum advantage.

For starters, here's a look at what conservatives truly stand for.

THE CONSERVATIVE MANIFESTO

Conservatives believe in faith-based wars, naked pyramids, the Confederate flag, gated communities, golden parachutes, and that what's good for Wal-Mart and Exxon Mobil is good for America.

Conservatives believe in fearmongering, gay-bashing, entitlement to power, patrio-fascist jingoism, more fearmongering, neo-Puritanism, giddy apocalypticism, and in building a bridge to the 19th century.

Conservatives believe in beautiful Hummers befouling spacious skies, amber waves of abstinent teens, and crowning thy good with estate tax cuts.

Conservatives believe in liberating people with cluster bombs.

Conservatives believe it is great sport to hunt pen-raised, wingless quail from a car.

Conservatives believe in dodging drafts, agitating for wars, smearing Democratic war veterans as unpatriotic, turning against wars when they become unpopular, and then accusing liberals of being spineless flip-floppers.

Conservatives believe they've just seen an apparition of the Virgin Mary in a grilled cheese sandwich.

Conservatives believe in taking away your sex toys.

Conservatives believe there is a War on Christmas, a War on Easter, a War on Independence Day, and possibly a War on Groundhog Day, too.

And more than anything else, conservatives believe that no matter how big a deficit you run, how badly you alienate allies, botch intelligence, or mismanage wars, it's still Clinton's fault.

Never underestimate the power of stupid people in large groups.

—Anonymous

A FIELD GUIDE TO THE CONSERVATIVE GENUS

Now it's time for you to meet the various species that make up the Republican Party's so-called "big tent." Familiarize yourself with this handy field guide so that you can quickly size up your opponent.

RAPTUREFARIANS

Religious fundamentalists and Christian evangelicals eagerly awaiting the Rapture and the End Times so that they may ascend to heaven and leave all godless, liberal heathens behind

AKA: Bible-thumpers, Christian Taliban, Hypo-Christians, Rapture Right

Natural habitat: Applebee's

Turn-ons: School prayer, megachurches, Middle East holy wars, forcibly inserting feeding tubes into vegetative patients

Turn-offs: Evolution, stem cells, abortion clinics, secular judges, watching gay newlyweds kiss

Likely to be seen: Passing out "True Love Waits" virginity pledge cards to teens in front of Wet Seal at the local mall

Would sooner be caught dead · than: Acknowledging the fact that teens who take abstinence pledges are five times more likely to engage in other non-biblically-sanctioned sex acts

ENRON-OMISTS

Conservative übercapitalists and apologists for big businesses who believe that trickle-down economics works wonders, job outsourcing is good for America, and large-scale fraud is simply an "accounting innovation"

AKA: Corporate-jet conservatives, country-club Republicans, corporate criminals

Natural habitat: Upper East Side of Manhattan, wealthy Washington, D.C. suburbs, minimum security jails

Turn-ons: The magic of the market (i.e., offshore tax shelters, no-bid contracts, cheap, illegal-immigrant labor)

Turn-offs: Welfare recipients, labor unions, trial lawyers, congressional subpoenas

Likely to be seen: Hiring a guy named "Karl" in Bangalore, India, to do your old job for half the cost

Would sooner be caught dead than: Serving time in prison after being convicted of conspiracy and fraud (see "Lay, Kenneth," 1942–2006)

BIG BRETHREN

Militant, chest-pounding überpatriots and authoritarian neofascists who believe war is peace, freedom is slavery, ignorance is strength, and 2 + 2 equals whatever Dick Cheney says it does

AKA: Hatriots, digital brownshirts, chicken-hawks, keyboard kommandos

Natural habitat: Talk-radio airwaves, online forums trolled by like-minded bottom feeders, the Attorney General's office

Turn-ons: The Patriot Act, groupthink, issuing anonymous death threats to liberal bloggers

Turn-offs: Free speech, logic, reason

Likely to be seen: Monitoring their grandmother's library records for signs of subversive activity

Would sooner be caught dead than: Actually serving in the military

GUNFEDERATES

Rednecks with Confederate flags on their pickup trucks; known to carry concealed weapons as last line of defense against liberal intellectuals and other would-be terrorists from the Northeast

AKA: Angry white men, rednecks, anti-Washington conservatives

Natural habitat: Rural backwaters and trailers everywhere

Turn-ons: *Guns & Ammo*, Hooters, televised fishing, Civil War reenactments where the South wins

Turn-offs: Social welfare parasites, big government they don't control

Likely to be seen: Stockpiling armaments to defend their Second Amendment rights in the event a Democrat becomes president

Would sooner be caught dead than: Defending the rest of the Bill of Rights

SPONGEBOB-OPHOBES

Social conservatives on the front lines of the culture wars who are fiercely committed to fighting the liberal/gay agenda; descended from Teletubsessive

Compulsives; characterized by all-consuming fear that the nation's children are taking sexual cues from a talking sponge, as opposed to, say, Paris Hilton

AKA: Traditional-values voters, culture warriors, white-breads

Natural habitat: Suburbs and exurbs containing no less than a 20:1 ratio of white Christians to ethnic and/or gay minorities

Turn-ons: Gay marriage bans, anti-sodomy laws, covering up partially naked statues with $8,000 drapes

Turn-offs: Hollywood, exposed nipples, sex acts not explicitly endorsed by Pat Robertson

Likely to be seen: In rehab to cure them of their homoerotic thoughts

Would sooner be caught dead than: Within a 100-mile radius of San Francisco

CRUSADOMASOCHISTS

Imperialistic neocons who hatch foreign policy schemes according to the strategic principles of Milton Bradley's *Risk*

AKA: Bush administration officials, Halliburton executives, *Weekly Standard* readers

Natural habitat: Undisclosed locations

Turn-ons: Bunker-busting nukes, waterboarding torture, Jack Bauer justice

Turn-offs: The UN, diplomacy, nation building, whiny liberal appeasers

Likely to be seen: Touring Iraq and touting the "good news" about peace and tranquility

Would sooner be caught dead than: Touring Iraq and touting the "good news" without flak jackets, armored vehicles, and a Marine battalion

OTHER CONSERVATIVE SPECIES YOU MAY ENCOUNTER

Evanbushicals: Conservatives who believe it is their divine right to be governed by Bushes

Texabitionists: Glad-handing, cowboy hat–wearing, neo-conquistadors who want to transform the rest of America into a suburb of Dallas–Fort Worth

Cro-Magnicons: Knuckle-dragging retro-conservatives who think all of America's problems would have been solved if only Strom Thurmond had been president

FOX Trotters: Smug, insufferable, True Believing conservatives who mindlessly parrot FOX News talking points under the misguided impression that they are fair-minded and chemically balanced

NASCARcrats: Slack-jawed, beer-soaked yahoos who derive as much endless amusement from taunting spineless liberal pansies as they do from watching cars drive around in circles

Anti-DC-stablishmentarians: Anti-Washington, states-rights libertarian-conservatives who love to rail against the federal government when they're not busy cashing their farm subsidies or feasting on federal pork

Kennebunkcons: Patrician WASPs, old-school conservative elites, and selected Skull & Bonesmen who summer in exclusive enclaves like Kennebunkport and sire petulant children who pretend they're from Texas

Hell is other people.

—Jean-Paul Sartre

How to Rate a Conservative's Partisan Intensity Quotient (PIQ)

In addition to being familiar with various conservative species, you will also need to gauge the extent of your opponent's partisan passion, inflexibility, or possible pathology. You can quickly determine your opponent's PIQ with this simple test. Award one point for each "yes" answer.

_____**1.** Do they send out long, expository, political emails?

_____**2.** Are the emails written in all caps, riddled with expletives, and sent to large distribution lists?

_____**3.** Do they own any books written by Rush Limbaugh or Bill O'Reilly, or any titles in the *Left Behind* series?

_____**4.** Do they own a copy of *Mein Kampf, The Protocols of the Elders of Zion*, or anything written by Ann Coulter?

_____**5.** Do they frequently repeat sound bites from FOX News?

_____**6.** Do they habitually quote from James Dobson sermons, Bush press conferences, or Mel Gibson DUI arrest tapes?

_____**7.** Have they ever chastised you for voting the wrong way?

_____**8.** Have they ever tried to get you to change your vote by bribing, blackmailing, shaming, or seducing you?

_____**9.** Do they frequently blame either Bill or Hillary Clinton for the world's problems?

_____**10.** Do they frequently blame either Bill or Hillary Clinton for things like inclement weather, the Yankees' losing streak, or their erectile dysfunction?

SCORING

9–10: SEVERE

Your opponent is an Unhinged Extremist (and likely armed). Approach with extreme caution.

7–8: HIGH

Your opponent is a Pugnacious Pitbull.
Hit 'em with everything you've got.

4–6: ELEVATED

Your opponent is a Dedicated Disciple.
You're in for a serious scuffle.

2–3: GUARDED

Your opponent is a Casual Combatant.
Crush 'em with overwhelming force.

0–1: LOW

Your opponent is a Guaranteed Pushover.
Show no mercy.

> The party of Lincoln and Liberty was transmogrified into the party of hairy-backed swamp developers and corporate shills, faith-based economists, fundamentalist bullies with Bibles, Christians of convenience, freelance racists, misanthropic frat boys, shrieking midgets of AM radio, tax cheats, nihilists in golf pants, brownshirts in pinstripes, sweatshop tycoons... Republicans: The No. 1 reason the rest of the world thinks we're deaf, dumb, and dangerous.
>
> —Garrison Keillor

FREQUENTLY ASKED QUESTIONS ABOUT CONSERVATIVES

Now that you know whom you're dealing with, it's time to get to the vexing questions about conservatives' peculiar behavior and seemingly inexplicable belief system.

Q. How does someone become a conservative anyway?

A. Generally speaking, it starts with sexual frustration, blossoms into anger, and pretty soon you want to cut taxes.

Q. Why are conservatives so mean-spirited?

A. Because wealthy, white, Christian males are tired of living in a society where all the breaks go to poor, gay, illegal immigrants.

Q. How can conservatives possibly believe the lies and bullshit they're spoon-fed by FOX News and right-wing radio? Do they have any concept of reality?

A. As Stephen Colbert once observed, "Reality has a well-known liberal bias."

Q. Is there a covert conspiracy among oil interests, Republican power brokers, and the military industrial complex to wage a war for global domination and control of the world's oil reserves?

A. No, they're fairly open about it.

Q. If Jesus preached peace, why are so many Bible-thumping Christians so gung-ho about war?

A. According to Christian apocalypticism, war in the Middle East will lead to Armageddon, which will lead to an epic battle between the antichrist and Jesus, after which will come one thousand years of peace and plenty. So as you can see, it's actually a well thought-out plan.

Q. Republicans come up with a lot of phrases like "compassionate conservatism," "leave no child behind," "clear skies," and "healthy forests" to disguise their destructive policies. Do they really expect people to buy that Orwellian nonsense?

A. As George W. Bush once said, "You can fool some of the people all the time, and those are the ones you want to concentrate on."

Q. How likely is it that I will be shot by an armed Republican?

A. Unless you are driving a hybrid car through the South with bumper stickers that say "Hillary for

President," "Amnesty for Illegals," "Just Gay Married," or "I've Come to Liberate You from Your Guns," it's fairly unlikely.

Q. How do conservatives sleep at night?

A. Like babies, actually, snuggly wrapped in a flag and comforted by the knowledge that someone else is fighting their wars of global conquest.

Conservatism is Bill Bennett lecturing you about self-denial, then rushing off to feed his slot habit at the casino. It's James Dobson telling you that children need regular beatings to stay in line. It's a superannuated nun rapping you on the knuckles so you won't think about your dirty parts. It's Jerry Falwell watching *Teletubbies* frame by frame to see if Tinky Winky is trying to turn him gay. Conservatism is everyone you never wanted to grow up to be.

—Paul Waldman

A Glimpse into the Conservative Utopia

Conservatives are working hard to build a society that realizes their dreams for total domination over America's political and cultural landscape. Whether they succeed or fail will depend on your commitment to derailing their plans. To illustrate what's at stake, here's a glimpse into America's possible future, should conservatives have their unfettered way with the country.

EXTRA! NEWSPAPER HEADLINES CONSERVATIVES WOULD LOVE TO SEE

❗ Republicans Simplify Tax Code; Taxpayers to Write Checks Directly to Halliburton

❗ FOX News Secures Exclusive Rights to Cover Battle of Armageddon

❗ Witch Trials Recommence; Hillary Clinton Proves Fully Combustible

❗ Schools Replace Math with Faith-based "Intelligent Counting"

- Supreme Court Outlaws Abortion; Exceptions Limited to Cases of Rape, Incest, or Impregnation of Congressional Staffers
- Entire Kennedy Clan Detained by Justice Department's Pre-crime Unit
- Global Warming Declared Hoax; White House Calls New Kansas Coastline "Naturally Occurring Phenomenon"
- U.S. Completes Moat of Fire to Keep Out Illegals, Low-Priced Prescription Meds
- Sean Hannity Raptured to Heaven during FOX News Broadcast; Alan Colmes, Left Behind, Still Can't Get Word in Edgewise
- Congress Set for IPO; Lawmakers to Be Publicly Traded on Stock Exchange

Don't think it could ever happen? Well, no one ever thought an untalented action hero, whose only prior accomplishment was liberating Mars, would become governor of the nation's largest state. Not to put too much pressure on you, but if you don't do your part to help frustrate their plans, the conservative utopians will have won.

★ **CHAPTER 3** ★

Can't We All Just Get Along?

As Americans, we must ask ourselves: Are we really so different? Must we stereotype those who disagree with us? Do we truly believe that ALL red-state residents are ignorant racist fascist knuckle-dragging NASCAR-obsessed cousin-marrying roadkill-eating tobacco juice-dribbling gun-fondling religious fanatic rednecks; or that ALL blue-state residents are godless unpatriotic pierced-nose Volvo-driving France-loving left-wing communist latte-sucking tofu-chomping holistic-wacko neurotic vegan weenie perverts?

—Dave Barry

L et's face it. Our great nation has been divided along fierce partisan lines ever since the days of our founding fathers, when even our finest powdered wig–wearing, silk stocking–strutting statesmen exchanged bitter recriminations over who was the bigger girlie-man.

With liberals and conservatives, Democrats and Republicans, and Blue Staters and Red Staters growing more polarized by the day, is there any hope left of finding common ground? The answer is yes. But before we get to that, let's first take stock of America's current state of disunion to discover exactly how deeply and ridiculously divided we have become.

A Day in the Life of Conservatives vs. Liberals

Conservatives and liberals may live in the same cities and breathe the same air, but they might as well be gliding along two separate planes of existence.

A Day in the Life of a Conservative	A Day in the Life of a Liberal
★ *7:00 a.m.*	
Wake up, flip on FOX News, pick outfit to match terror alert level	Wake up, wash down morning-after pill with hot cup of chai tea
★ *8:00 a.m.*	
Bible study	Pilates
★ *8:30 a.m.*	
Listen to Rush Limbaugh while idling in the Krispy Kreme drive-through line	Read *The New York Times* while sipping a latte at Starbucks
★ *9 a.m.*	
Arrive at work, force the community's last mom-and-pop shop out of business	Arrive at work at non-profit organization, sharpen pencil
★ *10 a.m.*	
Buy hundred-share lot of Bechtel stock in anticipation of war with Iran	Buy flock of chicks from Heifer International to donate to Kenyan village

A Day in the Life of a Conservative	A Day in the Life of a Liberal
★ *12 p.m.*	
Eat sandwich of leftover squab from weekend hunt, washed down with Bud	Enjoy bag lunch of braised fennel, watercress, and wheat grass juice
★ *3 p.m.*	
Gas up Hummer, reposition Confederate flag on window, clean homeless person off grille	Pump air in bicycle tires, lecture passing drivers about evils of internal combustion engine
★ *5 p.m.*	
Stop by drugstore for Viagra prescription, report suspicious-looking cashier to INS for deportation	Stop by drugstore for Prozac prescription, file punitive damage lawsuit after being told it isn't ready
★ *6 p.m.*	
Join the guys at Hooters to watch ESPN and ogle the waitstaff over a couple of pitchers	Join fellow tree huggers to block commuter traffic until the city agrees to build a "toad tunnel" allowing frogs to safely cross busy street

A Day in the Life of a Conservative	A Day in the Life of a Liberal
★ 7:30 p.m.	
Sit down to family dinner, discuss Pat Robertson's latest warning about how eating soy products can make you gay	Sit down to family dinner, discuss Sean Penn's recent op-ed on global security challenges of the 21st century
★ 8 p.m.	
Watch *The O'Reilly Factor* for fair and balanced news coverage	Watch *The Daily Show* for fair and balanced news
★ 10:00 p.m.	
Have missionary-position sex with spouse	Invite the neighbors over for a group orgy
★ 11 p.m.	
Recite prayers, await the Rapture	Smoke joint, fall asleep

> The Democrats are the party of government activism, the party that says government can make you richer, smarter, taller, and get the chickweed out of your lawn. Republicans are the party that says government doesn't work, and then get elected and prove it.
>
> —P. J. O'Rourke

Battle of the Bumper Stickers

There's no better illustration of the stark partisan split than the ideological battle that conservatives and liberals are waging every day on America's roadways.

Popular Liberal Bumper Stickers

★ The Rapture is *Not* an Exit Strategy
★ Bush Never Exhaled
★ Who Would Jesus Torture?
★ Would Someone Give Bush a Blowjob So We Can Impeach Him?
★ Stewart/Colbert 2008
★ Bush Is Listening. Use Big Words.

- ★ The Republican Party: Our Bridge to the 11th Century
- ★ Bush. Like A Rock. Only Dumber.
- ★ That's OK, I Wasn't Using My Civil Liberties Anyway
- ★ Think. It's Not Illegal Yet.
- ★ Killing for Peace Is Like Screwing for Virginity
- ★ At Least in Vietnam Bush Had an Exit Strategy

Popular Conservative Bumper Stickers

- ★ In Case of Rapture, This Car Will Be Unmanned
- ★ Ted Kennedy's Car Has Killed More People Than My Gun
- ★ If You're Gonna Burn Our Flag, Wrap Yourself in It First
- ★ Run, Hillary, Run (placed on front bumper)
- ★ Protest Noted. Now Shut the Hell Up!
- ★ My Honor Student Beat Up France
- ★ No Oil for Pacifists
- ★ Spotted Owls Taste Like Chicken
- ★ If Guns Kill People, Then Spoons Make Michael Moore Fat
- ★ Stop Global Whining
- ★ My SUV Can Beat Up Your Prius
- ★ Except for Ending Slavery, Fascism, Nazism, and Communism, War Has Never Solved Anything

Conservative, n: A statesman who is enamored of existing evils, as distinguished from the Liberal, who wishes to replace them with others.

—Ambrose Bierce

WHAT LIBERALS SAY VS. WHAT CONSERVATIVES HEAR

Most liberals and conservatives who have spent any time in the partisan trenches quickly discover that even basic attempts at communication can be utterly futile. Thanks to ingrained stereotypes, built-in defense mechanisms, and intense partisan conditioning, a liberal may say one thing, but a conservative is almost certain to hear something else. As you can see here, it's not pretty:

What liberals say: I'm tired of listening to religious nutcases and puritanical prudes trying to dictate what I do in the bedroom or what I can do with my body.

What conservatives hear: I'm a godless, amoral hedonist. Where's the nearest drive-through abortion clinic?

What liberals say: The media does not have a liberal bias.

What conservatives hear: The Earth is not round.

What liberals say: No war for oil.

What conservatives hear: My total comprehension of foreign policy is limited to four words.

What liberals say: We must fight for the people against the powerful.

What conservatives hear: The proletariat must rise up against the bourgeoisie, seize the means of production, and unite with the workers of the world.

What liberals say: Conservatives are all a bunch of warmongering, deficit-expanding, pollution-spewing, torture-sanctioning, civil liberty-seizing, New Orleans-abandoning, military-wrecking, Armageddon-yearning, fanatical bigots who have done more to destroy American democracy than Osama bin Laden ever dreamed.

What conservatives hear: I hate America, I hate freedom, and I hate myself.

WHAT CONSERVATIVES SAY VS. WHAT LIBERALS HEAR

There's no better luck on the flip side:

What conservatives say: We need to protect the sanctity of life, defend the sanctity of marriage, and teach our children the virtues of abstinence.

What liberals hear: We need to bomb abortion clinics, ban gay people, and fit our children with chastity belts.

What conservatives say: We need to reduce our dependency on foreign oil by pursuing oil exploration at home.

What liberals hear: We're going to drill for oil in the Alaskan wilderness, Yellowstone, and if necessary, Disney World.

What conservatives say: We need to crack down on illegal immigration.

What liberals hear: We need to crack down on illegal immigration after the cleaning crew at Wal-Mart finishes the night shift and Jorge mows my lawn.

What conservatives say: Family values are stronger in the red states.

What liberals hear: If you ignore the higher rates of divorce, teen pregnancy, and wife beatings, family values are stronger in the red states.

What conservatives say: Liberals are all a bunch of Hollywood-loving, gun-grabbing, stem cell–sucking, abortion-promoting, Michael Moore–worshipping, trial lawyer–humping, troop-slandering, terrorist-coddling defeatocrats who are hellbent on destroying America.

What liberals hear: Sieg heil!

I view America like this: 70-80 percent [are] pretty reasonable people that truthfully, if they sat down, even on contentious issues, would get along. And the other 20 percent of the country run it.

—Jon Stewart

COMMON ENEMIES WE CAN ALL AGREE TO HATE

OK, now that it's abundantly clear how hopelessly estranged and deranged the two warring sides have become, it's time to find that elusive common ground.

President Josiah Bartlet:
  We agree on nothing, Max.
Senator Max Lobell: Yes, sir.
Bartlet: Education, guns, drugs, school prayer, gays, defense spending, taxes— you name it, we disagree.
Lobell: You know why?
Bartlet: Because I'm a lily-livered, bleeding-heart, liberal, egghead communist.
Lobell: Yes, sir. And I'm a gun-toting, redneck son-of-a-bitch.
Bartlet: Yes, you are.
Lobell: We agree about that.
          —NBC's *The West Wing*

It's been said that what divides us as a country is not nearly as strong as what unites us. And what could unite us more than our common enemies? With that in mind, let us embark on the path to bipartisan unity by taking a moment to jointly revile some of the most odious miscreants, evildoers, and entities that liberals and conservatives can agree to hate.

You can, of course, never go wrong bashing the likes of Al Qaeda, Osama bin Laden, Kim Jong-il, Mahmoud Ahmadinejad, corporate criminals, and pedophiles. But if you really want to bond with conservatives, try trash-talking the following enemies of freedom, all of whom pose a more immediate threat to our collective sanity.

THE MEDIA

Conservatives complain that the media has a grotesque liberal bias. Liberals say the media practically gets down on its knees to service conservatives. Either way, you can count on the mainstream media to botch the facts and distort the truth in the race to get the story wrong first. Sure, there are some intrepid journalists doing important work, but as a whole, the establishment media is a brainless, sensationalistic, and unstoppable force that you can rely on to saturate the airwaves with wall-to-wall coverage of the latest missing white blonde girl, ignore the current genocidal war in Africa, blindly regurgitate partisan talking points, and, occasionally, make up stories out of whole cloth.

INTERNET SPAMMERS

There's a special molten cauldron on reserve in hell for the creators of Internet spam. These are the stalkers and perverts who sit around coming up with the radically moronic message headings that clog up your inbox, such as "Buff up your boner," "Let Yoda refinance your house," "Hot deals on Iraqi real estate," and "We have located several horny women in your area!" Forget Al Qaeda. Let's go after them.

GERALDO RIVERA

The mustachioed, sensationalistic television reporter was asked to leave Iraq after giving away U.S. troop positions, bragged about carrying a gun in Afghanistan that he wasn't afraid to use, claimed to be at the scene of a friendly fire incident when he was actually 300 miles away, and reportedly made an elderly Hurricane Katrina victim shoot multiple takes of him heroically rescuing her. He has also cried repeatedly on camera, often with little provocation. You won't find a better personification of everything that is insipid, self-aggrandizing, and soulless about celebrity journalism.

THE IRS

It's bad enough that our tax code is incomprehensible to intelligent man, but what really pisses everyone off is how ineptly and inconsistently our tax laws are enforced. The IRS is more likely to pester and probe the average working stiff than the average millionaire or the corporation that's squirreling away money in a Cayman Islands tax shelter. What's worse, every time you publicly mouth off against the IRS (say, in the pages of a book that names the IRS as an enemy of the people), you're almost sure to be audited.

TOM CRUISE

When not jumping up and down on couches, convincing Katie Holmes to carry his demon spawn, angrily impugning psychiatry, or making craptacular movies, Tom Cruise can be found touting a crackpot religion known as Scientology—an elaborately disguised pyramid scam created by a second-rate science fiction writer. It's based on the perfectly plausible belief that humans are descended from aliens who were frozen by an evil galactic overlord 75 million years ago, brought to Earth in a spaceship, dropped into volcanoes, and blown up with hydrogen bombs. Cruise is not only giving his fellow intergalactic travelers a bad name, but if he is not contained, he may continue to pose a clear and present danger to nubile Hollywood starlets throughout the universe.

CHAPTER 4

Basic Training

The definition of insanity is doing the same thing over and over again and expecting different results.

—Albert Einstein, attributed

There's a right way to engage conservatives in combat and a wrong way. The right way will enable you to make forceful arguments, win hearts and minds, and be greeted as a liberator. The wrong way will alienate your opponents, make them harden their position, and get you kicked out of public places.

Unfortunately, due to inadequate preparation and training—or sheer self-delusion—many people embark on the wrong path. To help you gird for battle and avert certain disaster, we'll show you in this chapter how to avoid key pitfalls, pick the right fights, and turn arguments to your advantage by following some basic rules of engagement.

THE SEVEN HABITS OF HIGHLY INEFFECTIVE PARTISANS

As with many things in life, we are often our own worst enemies. These seven habits are like kryptonite to the partisan warrior and must be painstakingly avoided.

1. BECOMING OVERLY EMOTIONAL

There's nothing more counterproductive to your cause—or costly to your metaphysical well-being—than becoming emotionally unraveled in the middle of an argument. If you're experiencing heart palpitations, developing blurred vision, or emitting cartoon steam from your nostrils while your opponent is sitting there stone-faced, you're not winning. Keep your rage in check at all times, and don't take things personally.

2. OOZING CONDESCENSION

Even if you believe you're talking to a breath-takingly misguided ignoramus, conceal it. If you patronize or belittle your opponents, they'll only dig in their heels. They'll also think that you're a sanctimonious, pompous wanker.

3. SPEWING HATEFUL INVECTIVE

There's nothing wrong with using hard-charging rhetoric and sharp-edged words, but if you want to be persuasive, you need to stop short of savage insults, epithets, and ridiculously inflammatory rhetoric (e.g., calling Republicans Nazis or crazed, totalitarian, bigoted fascists). Many media blovia-tors have built entire careers on hysterical dia-tribes, but that only works when you're preaching to the choir. Back on planet Earth, you'll never succeed in making a winning argument if you come off as a raging misanthrope.

4. INVENTING FACTS ON THE FLY

If you don't have the facts on hand to back up your argument, don't make them up. The facts will eventually catch up with you, and you'll be exposed as the fraud that you are.

5. LUMPING UNRELATED ISSUES TOGETHER

Nothing screams political sophistication like a protest to save the whales, get out of Iraq, shut down the IMF, stop the sale of genetically modified yams, and impeach Bush. Pick one issue or cause at a time and, for the love of logic, stay on message.

6. BECOMING CONSPIRATORIAL

It's tempting to believe there are sinister conservative forces engaged in grand, diabolical schemes (e.g., the Bush administration orchestrated 9/11, bin Laden is a CIA operative, and Dick Cheney is an evil cyborg). Don't bother going there. There are plenty of good arguments to make without bringing in the vast conspiracy of little green men on the grassy knoll. And besides, as anyone who has worked in government will tell you, the government isn't competent enough to pull off a decent conspiracy.

7. PICKING FIGHTS WITH OTHER LIBERALS

There's no denying that some liberals are utterly clueless and need a good smack in the head, but why do conservatives' dirty work for them? Nothing is more self-defeating than expending valuable energy tussling with another liberal while you both lose sight of the bigger picture. If you engage in partisan fratricide instead of focusing on the battles that really matter, you'll be helping the enemy divide and conquer.

How Woefully Ineffective Are You?

Now let's identify whether you're pre-disposed to any of the seven deadly habits. Answer these questions about how you would handle yourself in the following situations.

1. You're hanging out in your college dorm, passing around a bong, when one of your friends confesses that he's thinking of voting for a Republican in the next election. Do you:

_____A. Pour Drano into the bong and offer him another hit?

_____B. Gather every liberal you know, cue up *Fahrenheit 9/11*, and hold an immediate intervention?

_____C. Recruit a hot, liberal sorority girl to tie him up and reeducate him?

_____D. Ask him why stop there when he can go enlist in the military and spend his spring break patrolling the streets of Ramadi?

2. You're sitting at the Thanksgiving table, discussing Iraq, when your cousin Max invokes 9/11 eight times in a single sentence and says the war is payback for the terrorists who attacked us. Do you:

_____A. Denounce him as an idiotic fascist who would have made Hitler proud?

_____B. Launch into a thirty-minute soliloquy on historical discord in Mesopotamia?

_____C. Fling a drumstick at your brother Josh and then say cousin Max did it. Argue that he's been stockpiling poultry all night and that everyone must retaliate before he attacks again?

_____D. Explain that even President Bush was forced to admit Iraq had nothing to do with 9/11?

3. You make a comment to another parent at a PTA meeting about the importance of safe-sex education. She responds that kids should be taught abstinence only. Do you:

_____A. Play some Barry White and see how far you get?

_____B. Tell her you didn't realize she was a member of the Christian Taliban?

C. Ask if she's just bitter because she couldn't get laid in high school?

D. Point out there is no credible evidence that abstinence-only education works and that studies show it actually increases the rate of unsafe sex?

If you answered D to all of the above questions, you're ready to move on to the next section. If not, this may help explain why you haven't been winning many arguments lately (and possibly why you don't get invited to social functions anymore).

Your voice is like a jackal picking at my brain! I hate you! I hate who you are and what you do and how you sound and what you say! You're like a cancer on my life!

—Stephen Colbert, arguing with Steve Carell on *The Daily Show*

How Not to Be an Asshole

Tempted as you may be to blurt out obscenities, hurl insults, or pepper-spray your opponent, successful arguing strategy (and the laws of polite society) require that you employ more civilized tactics. This chart will show you how to channel your fury in a way that, while being admittedly less satisfying than, say, telling your opponent to go perform an anatomical sexual impossibility, will help encourage better diplomatic relations.

What You'll Be Tempted to Say	How to Translate That into Diplo-Speak
"Are you completely freaking insane?"	"I'm not sure I'm following the reasoning behind your argument."
"Did your lobotomy leave a scar?"	"Do you honestly believe that?"
"Which dark crevice of your ass did you pull that from?"	"How do you back up that claim?"
"Stupid inbred redneck."	"I can't identify with what you're saying."

What You'll Be Tempted to Say	How to Translate That into Diplo-Speak
"What do the demons say when they come for you at night?"	"How did you arrive at that conclusion?"
"Does your cable company only carry the FOX Network?"	"Let me suggest some news sources that report actual facts."
"Do I need to speak slower with fewer syllables?"	"I'm not sure we're communicating."
"I've never met a bigger phony in my life."	"Nice to meet you, Mr. Limbaugh."
"Isn't it great that we live in a country where even a total douche bag like yourself is free to utter whatever mindless drivel pops into his head?"	"You have a right to your opinion."

What You'll Be Tempted to Say	How to Translate That into Diplo-Speak
"I'd rather undergo waterboarding torture at the hands of Dick Cheney himself than listen to another word you have to say."	"I think we're going to have to agree to disagree."

THE TEN COMMANDMENTS OF PARTISAN WARFARE

Here is your guide to becoming a model partisan.

1. KEEP IT SIMPLE

A long-winded, complex, nuanced argument is a guaranteed ticket to disaster. As the great sage Dan Quayle once said, "Verbosity leads to unclear, inarticulate things." To be effective, you need to be able to fit your basic message on a bumper sticker.

2. PERSONALIZE THE ISSUE

Don't talk about issues in an abstract way. Persuade by talking in terms of how issues impact people, relate your own experiences, and highlight your opponents' self-interest (e.g., show them how Democratic policies mean better-paying jobs, cleaner air, or cheaper antipsychotic drugs).

3. FRAME THE ARGUMENT TO YOUR ADVANTAGE

Make your case by presenting each issue according to your beliefs and values, *not theirs*. Never, for example, let a sanctimonious conservative lecture you about what real American values are. If you let them frame the debate, they win (more on that later in this chapter).

4. FIND COMMON GROUND

Build your street cred with conservatives by bad-mouthing an annoying liberal—say, Jesse Jackson or Rosie O'Donnell. That way you'll defy stereotypes and demonstrate that your allegiances are not blind. Continue to rope them in by appealing to shared values and common interests before unleashing your Trojan horse–style sneak attack.

5. EXPOSE HYPOCRISY

Nothing undermines an argument faster than exposing hypocritical behavior, contradictory statements, and wholesale fakery—either on the part of your opponents or on the part of the politicians they're defending. There are few sights as satisfying as watching exposed hypocrites grasp at fig leaves to cover their shame.

6. EXUDE CONFIDENCE

Always project the courage of your convictions. Like bees and dogs, your opponent can smell fear and weakness. *How* you say something is just as important as *what* you say.

7. DON'T SERMONIZE

No one likes to be lectured to, and no one likes a self-righteous windbag. Ranting from atop your soapbox will only harden your opponent's position and make him or her more hostile. If you've made an enemy, you haven't won an argument.

8. MAKE YOUR OPPONENT LAUGH

Humor can be a potent weapon in political debate. Making humorous observations—and demonstrating an ability to laugh at yourself—will help disarm your opponents and keep them engaged. If funny isn't your thing, quote professional quipsters like Jon Stewart or unintentional comedians like George W. Bush.

9. BE OPEN-MINDED

It's the civility, stupid. Be prepared to listen respectfully and concede a point or two before moving in for the kill. You can learn a lot from people with whom you disagree—even those you believe to be outrageously misguided—and fine-tune your arguments in the process.

10. PICK BATTLES YOU CAN WIN

Don't expend too much energy trying to win over a staunch conservative. You'd have better luck trying to coax a rock to grow. Target the fence-sitters and the more easily converted. It's a strategy that has worked for religious missionaries for centuries, and it can work for you.

How to Frame the Debate Using Simple Jedi Mind Tricks

To win a political argument, you must control the terms of debate. If you let your adversary define the terms and frame the discussion, you lose. The concept of "framing" has been popularized by George Lakoff in his best-selling book, *Don't Think of An Elephant*. It's a fairly straightforward idea, but it's something that many liberals—how to put this gently—suck at.

Most conservatives have an intuitive sense of how to frame their arguments because they see liberalism as the root of the world's problems. Too often, liberals fall into the trap of accepting the premise of conservatives' arguments and arguing from a defensive posture, which only helps conservatives reinforce their points. That has to stop.

The key to successful framing is to 1. keep your eye on the big picture; 2. stay on the offensive; 3. don't get sidetracked trying to refute every conservative lie or distortion; 4. tie your argument into a broader narrative; and 5. never, under any circumstances—even if you're wired with electrodes, draped with a black hood, and ordered to balance on a box—let conservatives frame the debate on their own terms.

The handy thing about this approach is that it can be just as effective on the strong-willed as the weak-minded. Here are two examples of how to handle a debate on moral values; the first is badly botched, the second smartly framed.

Conservative blowhard: *I'll tell you what's wrong with this country—it's the breakdown of moral values. Hollywood and the cultural elite are pushing their liberal agenda on us, and now we've got condoms being dispensed like Pez in schools, abortions on demand, and gay nuptial orgies on our altars. Our very way of life is under assault by deviants.*

Untrained liberal: *Where do you get off trying to impose your ass-backward, repressed morality on the rest of us anyway? There's nothing immoral about safe sex, a woman's right to choose, or gay marriage, despite what Pat Robertson says God told him to tell you.*

Conservative blowhard: *Look, the point is, we need to restore traditional American family values. If* *this keeps up, pretty soon we're going to be allowing people to marry their pets. Is that the kind of society you want to live in?*

Untrained liberal: *It beats living in a society where nut jobs like you get to dictate sexual morality for the rest of us.*

Notice how the untrained liberal takes the bait and plays right into their hands by fighting on the conservative's turf? By being purely reactive, the untrained liberal loses from the outset. Contrast that to the smarter liberal, who seizes control of the discussion and reframes it around issues that work to her advantage.

Smarter liberal: *If we really want to promote moral values, let's talk about making health care a basic right, ensuring children don't go hungry, and providing equal access to a quality education. Let's talk about solving the global warming problem so we don't have to look for a new planet when the ice caps melt. Let's talk about the fact that we're running up debt faster than Bill Bennett at a Vegas craps table—and sticking our grandchildren with the bill. And how about avoiding* *war at all costs instead of launching bogus, faith-based crusades we can't win? I don't know about you, but I think those moral failings pose a greater threat to our way of life than the prospect of two middle-aged dudes filing a joint tax return.*

We'll show you how to frame more arguments in Chapter Seven, but you get the idea.

How to Avoid Unhinged Lunatics

There's nothing wrong with occasionally mixing it up with conservatives who have extreme views. It's the ones who have extreme personality disorders you should be concerned about. You know, those totally incapable of having an intelligent, thoughtful discussion about anything. They bicker instead of argue, rant instead of talk, and parrot instead of think.

These kinds of sociopaths can be found anywhere—ambushing perfect strangers at cocktail parties, accosting hapless victims at neighborhood barbecues, even holding entire families hostage at holiday time in hopes of spewing their claptrap with impunity.

There is no use wasting perfectly good oxygen arguing with these people. You'll be much better off—and cut down on your Xanax bills—if you focus your energies on reasonable people capable of passing a Field Sanity Test. Here's how to administer it:

★ Do they become instantly irate at the slightest of triggers? For example, if you say the word "Clinton," does their face turn visibly red and do their neck veins begin pulsating?

★ In place of the usual expletives, do they use "Dean," "Soros," "Pelosi," "Kennedy," or "Hollywood"?

★ Do they display a pathological fear of opposing viewpoints? For example, do they frequently tell you to "shut up," or in the preferred Dick Cheney vernacular, to "go fuck yourself"?

★ Are they prone to Tourette's-like outbursts in which they spasmodically denounce you as a "godless, hippie, terrorist-lover," "stupid, baby-killing feminazi," or "coastal-dwelling pervert"?

★ Do they wear their stupidity on their person? For example, are they sporting an "I Love Gitmo" button or still wearing a John Kerry "purple heart" Band-Aid left over from the 2004 election?

★ Do they have the same stock answer to everything? For example, do they frequently explain that liberals simply hate America, freedom, the flag, the troops, God, and kittens?

★ Do they host a show on FOX called *The O'Reilly Factor*?

If the conservative in question exhibits any of the above behavior patterns, he or she has failed the Field Sanity Test. Do yourself a favor—back away slowly and avoid these people as you would Bill O'Reilly's attempts to make sexual advances with a falafel (see Chapter Eight: The Conservative Hall of Shame). Nothing good will ever come of talking to them.

Anyone else is fair game.

★ **CHAPTER 5** ★

How to Win Friends While Antagonizing People

LUKE: Your thoughts betray you, Father. I feel the good in you, the conflict.

DARTH VADER: There is no conflict.

LUKE: You couldn't bring yourself to kill me before, and I don't believe you'll destroy me now.

DARTH VADER: You underestimate the power of the Dark Side. If you will not fight, then you will meet your destiny.

—*Star Wars: Return of the Jedi*

Everyone says you shouldn't argue politics in polite company. But where's the fun in that? You have to hone your combat skills somewhere. And who better to prey on than your friends and loved ones or the guy in the next cubicle?

Navigating these minefields, however, requires special training. To help you bait and baffle your adversaries (while avoiding interpersonal disaster), this chapter offers some essential "DOs" and "DON'Ts" for dealing with several potentially hazardous combat zones.

HOW TO SURVIVE FAMILY SPARRING MATCHES

For some families it's an annual ritual: Everyone is sitting around the dinner table, enjoying a lovely Thanksgiving meal and getting into the holiday spirit, when Uncle Blowhard says, "Speaking of things we have to be thankful for, every day I thank God for making Bush president."

Cousin Jessica takes the bait and says, "I can't believe you voted for that stupid, monkey-faced fascist." Pretty soon, the conversation descends into a back-and-forth volley of bitter pronouncements, like "Why don't you move to Canada!" and "If you're so gung-ho about war, go enlist!" At which point chairs are pushed back and dishes are cleared, while your mother weeps quietly in the corner.

The thing about arguing with family is, you're in it for the long haul. That gives you a little more leeway, so everyone knows they can push the envelope further than they would in other situations. For that reason, a few basic rules apply.

- ★ **DON'T** let Uncle Blowhard hold the dinner table hostage. Fact-check him right then and there using the Internet browser on your BlackBerry or cell phone. Counter him point-for-point, fire off contradictory statistics, and apply duct tape as needed. Remember, conservatives hate facts. They get in the way of sweeping generalizations. It's like sunlight to a vampire.

- ★ **DON'T** proselytize to your children about your politics; they'll just rebel. First they'll start experimenting by reading conservative blogs privately, and then progress to social use of GOP talking points. The next thing you know they'll have developed a habitual dependency on conservative dogma, for which there may be no rehabilitation.

★ **DON'T** try to get in the last word with a conservative loved one at his or her own funeral. It comes off as insensitive to stand over a deceased conservative saying, "I bet you wish you'd had universal healthcare now," "Guess that estate tax isn't so important where you're going," or "Let me know what Jesus has to say about trickle-down economics when you're panhandling in hell."

★ **DO** crack jokes to disarm your opponents and lull them into a false sense of complacency. Keep an ample supply of alcohol at the ready, or better yet, ply them with coffee or Red Bull (people who are wired on caffeine are more susceptible to persuasion, according to an actual scientific study).

★ **DO** attempt to recruit impressionable family members to your side, particularly when they're young; for example, give your seven-year-old nephew a copy of the complete *Star*

Wars saga on DVD and explain how Jedis are Democrats and the evil Sith Lords are Republicans—as identified by their blue and red light sabers.

★ **DO** quote the Bible when arguing with your religious relatives, as beating zealots with their own stick can be a blissful religious experience. Be sure to bring up the parts they choose to gloss over, like "love thy neighbor," "the meek shall inherit the Earth," and "thou shall not molest thine underage page."

WHAT TO DO IF YOU'RE SLEEPING WITH THE ENEMY

Love makes people do crazy things, and chief among them is dating (or even marrying) your political enemy. Many households have their own partisan divides. He listens to Rush Limbaugh; she listens to NPR. He decides who to vote for based on the candidate he'd most like to drink beer with; she goes with the person she'd rather trust performing brain surgery. He's a serpent-headed Democratic strategist known as the Ragin' Cajun; she's a sharp-tongued Republican strategist and confidant of Dick Cheney.

Some mixed couples manage to coexist in a state of harmony. For others, it ends with a restraining order. Consider the case of one couple in Georgia who made headlines after the woman informed her boyfriend, a Marine recruit, that she was leaving him *and* voting for John Kerry. That's when he tried to stab her repeatedly with a screwdriver. "You'll never live to see the election," he told her before officers subdued him with a taser gun.

Well, there was no sex for fourteen days.

—California Governor Arnold Schwarzenegger, on how his wife, Maria Shriver (of Kennedy clan fame), reacted after he gave a speech praising President Bush at the 2004 Republican Convention

To help you remain faithful to both your beliefs and your significant other (while keeping yourself out of jail), here are a few pointers.

★ **DON'T** engage in any sort of political discussion with your opposite-ideological partner if you're hoping to get laid afterward. Wait until after the sex. Five minutes is not going to kill you. Remember, if you're having sex correctly, you won't have the energy for the argument to get out of hand. (If perchance the sex was unprotected, now would be a good time to discuss a woman's right to choose.)

★ **DON'T** resort to amateurish passive-aggressive behavior, such as lining the birdcage with your honey's absentee ballot. Instead, take it up a notch—host a PETA party at the house and release his prized bird back to nature.

★ **DON'T** let resentments fester; if you're still bitter about the volunteer work he did for the Quayle 2000 campaign, it's time to let it go.

★ **DON'T** kid yourself; if you discover a robe, a hood, and a stockpile of ammunition, pack up the kids and head for the nearest blue state.

★ **DO** keep political banter light. Ask yourself, WWJSD (What Would Jon Stewart

Do?) and try to maintain a sense of ironic self-detachment.

★ **DO** tease your significant other about how he is really a Democrat deep down. (How else to explain that he stopped watching *ER* after George Clooney left or the fact that Arianna Huffington is on his celebrity sex list?)

★ **DO** consider withholding sex to make a political point, but only if you're capable of holding out (guys, please skip to the next tip). If that doesn't work, try withholding gadgets or restricting his PlayStation or TiVo privileges.

★ **DO** agree on a safeword to signal when you've reached your limit, like people do with S&M; if he's extolling the virtues of repealing the capital gains tax and you just can't take it anymore, shout out "eightball," "bananas," or "Greenspan" and take a time-out.

HOW TO MANAGE WORKPLACE SQUABBLES

During the course of their adult lives, most Americans are doomed to spend about one-third of every waking hour toiling in the workplace. Whether you're looking for a political argument or not, you're bound to find yourself mixing it up with a conservative colleague sooner or later. Because workplace arguments can be a serious occupational hazard, here are some tips that will help you serve your partisan cause while holding onto your job at the same time.

- ★ **DON'T** get into a political spat with your boss unless you have some sort of leverage, like illicit intern photos or stock manipulation documents. In that case have a go at it: Nothing is more fun than blackmailing your boss into wearing a "Lick Bush" muscle-T on casual Friday.

- ★ **DON'T** be a stalker, like that guy in accounting who's always cornering people, ranting about the evils of the military-industrial complex, and trying to get you to read his MySpace blog; no one likes that guy.

- ★ **DON'T** plaster your workspace with annoying propaganda or signage (e.g., stickers that say "U.S. Out of My Uterus"—especially if you don't have a uterus—or that photo of you and Dennis Kucinich writhing in the mud at Burning Man). It signals you're either desperate for attention or huffing liquid paper. In either case, your coworkers will avoid you. Note: This "don't" is even more important if you share your cubicle with your Beanie Baby™ collection and photos of your six cats.

★ **DO** form alliances with like-minded colleagues; a coordinated assault around the watercooler by a coalition of the willing is always better than going it alone. You can even pass resolutions and impose sanctions against rogue departments.

★ **DO** consider playing psychological warfare; convince a conservative colleague that you're actually a conservative too, win his or her trust, and then at a crucial moment— say, right before Election Day—express your total disillusionment with the Republican Party and convince your colleague to join you in abandoning ship.

★ **DO** turn a difference of opinion into a friendly wager. If you win a bet about Democrats prevailing in the upcoming election, for example, your coworker has to agree to wear a tie with donkeys on it at all staff meetings for one year.

★ **DO** make sure to participate in departmental birthday celebrations. You'll get free cake, and when the conservative's card is passed around, you can write an impassioned birthday wish and sign it "John Edwards." Who isn't going to vote for someone who wrote nice things on their birthday card?

HOW TO CLASH WITH PERFECT STRANGERS

A few days after the 2004 presidential election, a pugnacious liberal posted the following anonymous message on Craigslist.org in Washington, D.C.: "I would like to fight a Bush supporter to vent my anger. If you are one, [and] have a fiery streak, please contact me so we can meet and physically fight. I would like to beat the shit out of you."

Another Craigslist poster offered a similar proposition: "Any of you Republicans want to fight? Street brawl, bodies only, no weapons. I will not be merciful. I'm sick of this tough-guy shit. Let's see what you got."

Going around and picking fights with strangers is generally not recommended. However, there are a few situations where *verbally* mixing it up with strangers may be warranted, perhaps even imperative. Here are a few guidelines.

- ★ **DON'T** antagonize anyone who may be able to take advantage of you in a compromising situation, such as your hairstylist, skydiving instructor, plastic surgeon, anesthesiologist, or the guy making your burrito.

- ★ **DON'T** attempt to enter a political discussion with anyone while high on marijuana. Nothing undermines your credibility like being called a liberal hippie stoner when you *are* a liberal hippie stoner.

- ★ **DON'T** get into an argument with the conservative sitting next to you on an airplane. There won't be enough barf bags on hand to stop him from hyperventilating and sucking up all the oxygen. And worse, you'll have no exit strategy.

★ **DO** feel free to mix it up with petition gatherers, pamphleteers, and other partisan stalkers; the longer you hold them hostage, the less time they'll have to disperse their propaganda.

★ **DO** crash a "Value Voters Summit," "Justice Sunday" rally, or any other confab of religious conservatives where you can taunt the Christian faithful; if you can provoke a violent outburst from just one Bible-bearing messenger of God, it will make for amusing news coverage.

★ **DO** feel free to track down the Republicans responsible for the annoying and incessant "robocalls" you received telling you that the Democrat on the ballot drinks the blood of children. Find the home phone numbers for anyone involved, anonymously post them on every liberal blog, sit back, and enjoy the turn of the karmic wheel.

HOW TO PROPERLY ENGAGE IN INTERNET FLAME WARS

If you've never been denounced as a bedwetting, fascist, crack-addicted, terrorist crybaby by dozens of people you've never met, you've never experienced the joys of an Internet flame war. For the uninitiated, this is where you post messages in any type of online forum and engage in a flaming back-and-forth war of words that would generally be considered unacceptable in polite society.

There are two key advantages in engaging in this type of political discourse: 1. You get to deploy all the anti-conservative epithets and denunciations that have been swirling in your mind; and 2. it's all anonymous, which means there's no need to lose any sleep over the taunts or threats that will inevitably be issued against you.

If you plan to get involved in a flame war, here are a few things to keep in mind. Note that some of the tips here run counter to the advice offered elsewhere in the book. That's the whole point of flame wars. It is the Internet, after all. Normal rules of decorum need not apply.

★ **DON'T** call your opponent a Nazi. That's so 20th century. Instead use terms like digital brownshirt, cyber jihadist, Fascist troll, and, where appropriate, batshit-crazy, genocidal douche bag.

★ **DON'T** ever provide any real information about yourself. It's more fun to pretend to be someone you're not—a mid-level Homeland Security official, for example, who is carefully monitoring everything they're saying.

★ **DON'T** get overly worked up or spend too much time flaming. If you're missing meals or forgetting to shower, you've got a problem. That's valuable time you could use for more productive pursuits, like trying to hack Sean Hannity's "Hannidate" conservative dating Web site or signing up the staff of National Review Online for military recruiting emails.

★ **DO** feel free to invent your own facts. If pressed for evidence, simply create your own Wikipedia entry to support your arguments. There are plenty of Wikipidiots out there who will believe anything they read on the Net.

★ **DO** take high personal offense to anything you can. Explain, for example, that you lost an arm, a leg, and an eye in the War on Christmas and you're outraged by his callous insensitivity. Inform them that you've been slandered and that they'll be hearing from your lawyer.

★ **DO** demonstrate that you are on the cutting edge of Internet discourse by using expletives such as "asshat," "assclown," and "ignoranus." Bonus points: If you use the number "3" instead of the letter "e" and "P" in place of "O," you'll confuse the piss out of them and let them know they've been "Pwn3d! LOL!"

CHAPTER 6

Advanced Battle Tactics

The enemy isn't liberalism. The enemy isn't conservatism. The enemy is bullshit.

—Lars-Erik Nelson

To triumph in battle, you need to be prepared to deal with devious adversaries. As you probably well know, many conservatives are highly skilled in the dark arts of manipulation. They bullshit with abandon and commit grotesque crimes against logic as a force of habit.

In this chapter, we'll show you how to cut through that nonsense. We'll help you hone your

Bullshit Detector, anticipate bogus lines of attack, and exploit weaknesses in your opponents' arguments so you can force them to engage in a more honest debate—or shut them up entirely.

To round out your training, we'll provide some advanced-level tips for seasoned combatants and show you how to turn even the bleakest of situations into a moral victory.

HOW TO DETECT BULLSHIT

Let's state the obvious. Conservatives love to bullshit. We're not just talking about the professionals who sell us bogus wars or promise us "fair and balanced" news. Your average conservative on the street is skilled at slinging it too.

To combat bullshit, it's important to first define what it is and what makes it so insidious. "Bullshit is a greater enemy of the truth than lies are," says Harry Frankfurt, who literally wrote the book *On Bullshit*. A bullshitter, Frankfurt says, is distinguished by the fact that he couldn't care less about whether what he is saying is true. He has a completely different agenda. A bullshitter is mainly concerned with trying to wow, distract, or manipulate his audience, and he'll simply cherry-pick facts or make up things to fit his needs.

That's why bullshitters are such menaces to society. Their total lack of regard for the truth gives them free rein to manipulate people willy-nilly, so long as no one calls them on it.

They also have one thing in common: They're trying to conceal something. To help you calibrate your Bullshit Detector, here's a guide to the various bullshitting life forms that you are likely to encounter and what they are trying to hide.

THE KNOWLEDGE SUPREMACISTS

What they do: They attempt to dazzle their audiences with their sheer volume of knowledge on any given topic. Their goal is to use that knowledge as a trump card to assert their superior opinions, based on having access to information you are lacking.

What they're hiding: Their intellectual inferiority complex.

THE CREDENTIAL FALSIFIERS

What they do: They claim to have unique life experiences or qualifications that you don't, which therefore validate their views and negate yours. For example, they may refer to their military training and combat experience when it turns out that all they ever did was play paintball.

What they're hiding: The fact that they're average and ill-informed.

THE FACT SPINNERS

What they do: They present you with the "straight facts," which, on closer examination, turn out to be wrong, distorted, taken out of context, or spun to suit their agenda. When faced with inconvenient facts, they create a smokescreen of doubt by either questioning the source (e.g., rejecting anything reported by the so-called "liberal media") or declaring the facts open to debate.

What they're hiding: That they no longer know the difference between fact and fiction, and worse, they don't care.

THE "TRUTHINESS" TELLERS

What they do: They cling to the truths that come straight from their gut, rather than from reality. As defined by comedian Stephen Colbert, "truthiness" refers to an individual's preference for believing in what he or she wishes to be true rather than what is known to be true.

What they're hiding: Their utter terror of reality.

THE BULLSHIT ACOLYTES

What they do: They perpetuate right-wing spin through empty sloganeering and mindless repetition of GOP talking points crafted by Bill O'Reilly, Rush Limbaugh, Sean Hannity, and their many shrieking clones.

What they're hiding: The fact that they can't think for themselves.

How to Trip Up a Bullshitter

Good bullshitters can be hard to spot, but you may be able to trip them up by their failure to answer basic questions or inability to support their claims.

Next time you smell the stink, take the following steps:

1. Hit them with simple questions, such as "How do you know that?"; "How can you prove that?"; or if you've got a firm fix on the facts: "How do you account for the fact that FOX News, the *Wall Street Journal*, and Jesus himself completely contradict everything you just said?"

2. If you suspect they're just blindly spewing rhetoric or unthinkingly parroting right-wing spin, challenge them to provide specifics. For example, make them explain exactly how Democrats are conspiring with Al Qaeda, specifically how CNN is guilty of liberal bias, or precisely how Nancy Pelosi plans to turn everyone gay.

3. As they grasp to substantiate their claims, watch for telltale signs of lying, such as lack of eye contact, a scratch to the nose or chin, compulsive lip-licking, dilated pupils, or sweating through their personally monogrammed shirt. Consider responses such as "I saw it on the Drudge Report," "I heard it in church," or "Because Bush said so" to be inadequate defenses.

4. Call them on their deceit, show them where they went wrong, and suggest that they leave the

bullshitting to trained professionals, like Karl Rove armed with talking points, Rush Limbaugh armed with pain pills, or Dick Cheney armed with . . . well, just armed.

HOW TO SPOT LOGICAL FALLACIES

If you've ever been part of an argument that feels disingenuous, grossly oversimplified, rigged against you, or which makes no earthly sense, then you've probably encountered a logical fallacy. They're the three-legged stools of faulty reasoning that conservatives rely on to prop up many of their ridiculous ideas.

Some conservatives deliberately use logical fallacies to play manipulative mind games, while others may inadvertently stick a finger in the eye of reason. Whatever the case, learning to recognize common logical fallacies—and calling your opponent on them—will help you to immediately deflate many bogus lines of attack. Or, if you're feeling Machiavellian, you can use these techniques to pull a fast one on an unwitting opponent.

FALSE CHOICE

Offering only two options for consideration when there are clearly other valid choices

Example: "If we give up the fight in the streets of Baghdad, we will face the terrorists in the streets of our own cities." —George W. Bush

STRAW MAN

Oversimplifying, exaggerating, caricaturing, or otherwise misrepresenting your position without regard to fact. In doing this, your opponent sets up a figurative straw man that he can easily knock down to prove his point.

Example: "Conservatives saw the savagery of 9/11 in the attacks and prepared for war; liberals saw the savagery of the 9/11 attacks and wanted to prepare indictments and offer therapy and understanding for our attackers." —Karl Rove

AD HOMINEN

Leveling a personal attack in an attempt to discredit an argument rather than addressing the argument itself

Example: "Feminism was established to allow unattractive women easier access to the mainstream of society." —Rush Limbaugh

HASTY GENERALIZATION

Jumping to a far-reaching conclusion based on scant evidence or forming a stereotype based on a single flimsy example or two

Example: "Liberals hate America, they hate flag-wavers, they hate abortion opponents, they hate all religions except Islam, post-9/11. Even Islamic terrorists don't hate America like liberals do. They don't have the energy. If they had that much energy, they'd have indoor plumbing by now." —Ann Coulter

SLIPPERY SLOPE

Leaping to wild, sometimes inexplicable conclusions—going, say, from Step One to Step Two and then all the way to Step Ten without establishing any discernible connection. By using this kind of leapfrog logic, a person can come to any conclusion he damn well pleases.

Example: "All of a sudden, we see riots, we see protests, we see people clashing. The next thing we know, there is injured or there is dead people. We don't want to get to that extent." —Arnold Schwarzenegger, on the dangers posed by gay marriage

THE BANDWAGON APPEAL
Demonstrating that an argument is valid based on the fact that it is popularly accepted or because "everyone is doing it"

Example: "All the polls say that most Americans believe as I do: that the traditional signs of Christmas are a good thing. So leave them alone, okay?" —Bill O'Reilly, making the case for allowing nativity scenes in public schools

APPEAL TO FEAR
Preying on people's fears in an attempt to skirt any need for evidence or analysis about an issue

Example: "We don't want the smoking gun to be a mushroom cloud." —Condoleezza Rice, arguing the case for war with Iraq

SHIFTING THE BURDEN OF PROOF

Presenting an argument as commonly accepted truth, failing to support it with any evidence, and then forcing you to prove otherwise. This tactic is employed out of laziness or to mask the reality that the facts are not on your opponent's side.

Example: "I think the burden is on those people who think he didn't have weapons of mass destruction to tell the world where they are." —Ari Fleischer, on Saddam Hussein's alleged WMDs

FALSE CAUSE

This fallacy, known among logic buffs as *post hoc ergo propter hoc*, is based on the assertion that because

A Fallacious Quiz

Which logical fallacy does David Letterman slap down in this exchange with Bill O'Reilly over whether Iraq was working with Al Qaeda?

O'Reilly: It isn't so black and white, Dave—it isn't "We're a bad country. Bush is an evil liar." That's not true.

Letterman: I didn't say we were a bad country. I didn't say he was an evil liar. You're putting words in my mouth, just the way you put artificial facts in your head!

Answer: Strawman

one action or event occurs and is followed by another, the first must have caused the second.

Example: "Guns have little or nothing to do with juvenile violence. The causes of youth violence are working parents who put their kids into daycare, the teaching of evolution in the schools, and working mothers who take birth control pills."
—Tom DeLay, on causes of the Columbine High School massacre

"STRATEGERY" FOR THE ADVANCED COMBATANT

Your conservative opponents are likely to rely on deceitful and underhanded tactics, so you'll need to stay one step ahead. Here are a few winning plays and ploys you can use to outmaneuver your opponent and give yourself maximum advantage in any political argument.

ANTICIPATE YOUR OPPONENTS' ARGUMENTS

You can gain a tactical advantage by familiarizing yourself with your opponents' arguments and understanding why they make them.

Your mission: You'll have to occasionally brave the unspeakable horrors of reading their crazy magazines, opinion columns, and blogs, listening to their talk-radio squawkers, watching the Faux News channel, and even subjecting yourself to the torture of a Bush news conference or State of Denial address.

Upshot: If you're not acquainted with the latest fashions in conservative thought, you won't fully appreciate how insane they actually are.

ASK POINTED QUESTIONS THAT WILL BOX IN YOUR OPPONENT

One of the most effective arguing techniques, utilized by lawyers and others skilled in the persuasion arts, simply involves posing a series of questions. It's known as the Socratic method, and it's easy to employ.

Your mission: Start by getting your opponents to answer broad questions about their beliefs, and then as you narrow down to the specific issue at hand, look to expose inconsistencies or contradictions. For example, ask if fiscal responsibility is a core value of conservatism. Ask if it would be fiscally responsible to increase your spending at a time when you're running up huge credit card debt. Then ask if the huge, Republican-created deficits are fiscally responsible.

Upshot: You make your opponents defeat themselves.

ANSWER THE QUESTION YOU WISH YOU'D BEEN ASKED

Many conservatives will ask you dumb, leading, or nonsensical questions to try and trap you. You don't have to play that game when you can recast the question in a way that works to your advantage—a simple little trick politicians use every day.

Your mission: When a conservative asks something like, "How can you be for abortion but against the death penalty?" recast it by saying, "I wonder how someone who is supposedly pro-life can be pro-death, especially when it comes to supporting wars that claim innocent lives."

Upshot: You remain on the offensive, frame the debate as you want to, and avoid conservatives' attempts to place you in a rhetorical straightjacket.

How to Argue Like a Conservative in Fourteen Easy Steps

If you've ever wondered why arguing with conservatives feels a lot like banging your head against a wall, it's because their debating strategy typically follows this basic pattern:

1. Invoke 9/11
2. Blame the liberal media
3. Impugn liberals' patriotism
4. Blame Clinton
5. Make thinly-veiled racist comment
6. Blame Hollywood
7. Feign indignation about flag-burning, the war on Christmas, or some other bogus issue
8. Blame immigrants
9. Misquote the Bible
10. Invoke 9/11 again
11. Complain about paying taxes
12. Dismiss all liberal arguments as conspiratorial
13. Change the subject
14. Rinse and repeat

NEVER USE CONSERVATIVES' WORDS

Conservatives love to use phrases like "death tax," "partial-birth abortion," "marriage penalty," and "tax relief" to spin their various positions. The worst thing you can do is to repeat them. As conservative language guru Frank Luntz says, "When you use the words of your opposition, you are basically accepting their definition and therefore their conclusion."

Your mission: When a conservative refers to permanently repealing the "death tax" (also known as the "estate tax"), refer to it as an effort to "protect Paris Hilton's inheritance." When they refer to "alternative interrogation techniques," call it "torture." When they talk about "cut and run," tell them what we really ought to do is "stop and think."

Upshot: By beating your opponents at their own word game, you put them on the defensive while exposing the lie behind their inane babble.

USE WEDGE ISSUES

For years, Republicans have been talking up wedge issues like abortion, gay marriage, flag burning, and gun control to prey on the liberals' biases, polarize the electorate, and peel off would-be Democratic voters.

Your mission: Talk up left-wing wedge issues, like Republicans' failure to fund life-saving stem cell research, sanctioning of torture, or their love affair with outsourcing.

Upshot: By doing unto them as they have done unto others, you'll keep your opponents on the defensive and beat them at their own game.

SHINE A LIGHT ON CONSERVATIVE WINGNUTS

You know the bar scene in *Star Wars* with all the bizarre-talking, freakish-looking alien creatures and miscreants? Those are the kinds of people who caucus with conservatives.

Your mission: Make a point of highlighting every crazy Pat Robertson fatwa, every outrageous Ann Coulter slander, or every deviant Bill O'Reilly sexual fetish to illustrate the true face of conservatism (see Chapter Eight: The Conservative Hall of Shame).

Upshot: The more you tie conservatism to its most unhinged extremists, the more unsavory the entire conservative philosophy becomes for nonpsychotic adherents. All you need to do is shine the light and back away.

> I argue very well. Ask any of my remaining friends. I can win an argument on any topic, against any opponent. People know this, and steer clear of me at parties. Often as a sign of their great respect, they don't even invite me.
>
> —Dave Barry

How to Win When You Can't Win Them Over

As a passionate partisan who's determined to convert conservatives to your way of thinking, you want what anyone would want: to watch them grovel on their knees as they recant their beliefs and praise you for showing them the path to salvation.

The odds of that happening, of course, are about as good as President Bush volunteering his own daughters to go fight his war in Iraq.

The reality is that you can do everything right, make flawless arguments, and still find yourself getting nowhere, your head throbbing with that dull concussive feeling that comes from butting your head against a wall of steel-reinforced ignorance. Fortunately, there are several other important ways in which you can still declare victory when you haven't won them over. You can unfurl your "Mission Accomplished" banner if you succeed in doing any of the following.

HUMILIATE YOUR OPPONENT

If you can undercut your opponent's arguments while making him look foolish in the process, you may not win a convert, but you can emancipate yourself—and perhaps a few grateful bystanders— from their bullshit.

BREAK STEREOTYPES

You can do a lot to mess with conservatives' minds simply by presenting yourself as a thoughtful liberal who cares about her country and makes intelligent, reasoned arguments. That way, the next time they try to say that all liberals are a bunch of brainless, knee-jerk, tree-hugging flakes, the wholly unfamiliar part of their brain known as their conscience will alert them to the fact that they're lying. Some conservatives obviously won't have a problem with this, but others will be forced to make accommodations to the unwanted intrusion of reality.

SHAKE THEIR CONFIDENCE IN THE REPUBLICAN PARTY

You may not be able to persuade people that their views are wrong, but you may be able to show them that their party is not representing their views. You can score a victory by highlighting the many ways in which the Republican Party has abandoned core conservative principles such as limited government, fiscal restraint, and not building a foreign policy based on delusional, apocalyptic fantasies. To paraphrase Ronald Reagan, show them that they haven't left the party, but their party has left them.

SOW YOUR OPPONENT WITH SEEDS OF SELF-DOUBT

If your opponent gives you everything he's got and then finds himself trapped under the weight of his own inadequacy—making fruitless counterarguments or being reduced to speechlessness—that's a good time to walk away. Let him fester in his own silent insufficiency. One day those seeds may bloom into giant flowers of debilitating self-doubt.

WIN OVER THE CROWD

When you're arguing with a conservative in front of other people—at a dinner party, for example—you can score a major victory simply by making superior arguments. Your goal is to appear more knowledgeable, more reasonable, and more logical, while exposing your opponent as ill-prepared, hypocritical, or simply clueless. Do that, and it doesn't matter whether you win over your adversary because you will have won the crowd.

PREVAIL IN A WAR OF ATTRITION

You may not be able to bring someone around overnight, but with patience and persistence, and possibly with the help of enough alcohol, you may eventually break your opponent down and get her to admit the folly of her ways—or at least stop voting for Republicans.

★ ★ ★ ★ ★ ★ ★ ★ ★ ★ ★ ★ ★ ★

How to Argue Like a Spin Doctor

In the film *Thank You for Smoking*, a tobacco lobbyist (Nick) and his son (Joey) discuss arguing strategy:

Nick: Let's say that you're defending chocolate, and I'm defending vanilla. Now, if I were to say to you 'Vanilla is the best flavor ice cream,' you'd say . . .

Joey: 'No, chocolate is.'

Nick: Exactly. But you can't win that argument. So, I'll ask you, 'So you think chocolate is the end-all and be-all of ice cream, do you?'

Joey: It's the best ice cream. I wouldn't order any other.

Nick: Oh. So it's all chocolate for you, is it?

Joey: Yes, chocolate is all I need.

Nick: Well, I need more than chocolate. And for that matter, I need more than vanilla. I believe that we need freedom and choice when it comes to our ice cream, and that . . . is the definition of liberty.

Joey: But that's not what we're talking about.

Nick: Ah. But that's what I'm talking about.

Joey: But . . . you didn't prove that vanilla's the best.

Nick: I didn't have to. I proved that you're wrong, and if you're wrong, I'm right.

Joey: But you still didn't convince me.

Nick: I'm not after you. I'm after them (*pointing to the public at large*).

★ **CHAPTER 7** ★

Kick-Ass Arguments: A Step-By-Step Guide

If you've got them by the balls, their hearts and minds will follow.

—Anonymous

N

ow that you're primed for battle, it's time to get down and dirty and argue the issues. Here you'll find shorthand guides to help you win arguments on a fistful of key issues at the core of today's left–right debate. We'll show you how to frame arguments to your advantage, hammer home compelling points, slap down your opponents' counterarguments, and bludgeon them with damning facts.

As a general rule—and to protect your own sanity—it's best to steer clear of radioactive issues like abortion, God, guns, and gays, which, let's face it, propel conservatives into instant histrionics. That's not to say you can't make potent arguments on those issues; they're just not your best cards to play. You'll be better off going for the jugular on issues like taxes and terrorism, where you can have a more sober-minded debate.

While we can't guarantee victory in every case, we can show you how to keep your opponents on the defensive and upend their reality. You'll need to draw on your newly acquired skills to flesh out the details and deflect your opponents' specific attacks, but consider this a basic primer to steer you in the right direction.

GLOBAL WARMING: WHY IT'S AN ISSUE OF SECURITY AND MORALITY

STEP 1: FRAME YOUR ARGUMENT

Debunk the myth that the global warming threat is overblown and demonstrate how, if we keep listening to conservatives, we could be looking at a grim future (picture *Mad Max* meets *Waterworld* meets *Apocalypse Now*).

STEP 2: MAKE YOUR CASE

★ The scientific debate is over. Man-made greenhouses gases are causing global temperatures to rise at a rate that should be every bit as alarming as the exponential increase of Exxon's profits.

★ While liberals and progressives seek urgent and sensible solutions to head off a planetary cataclysm, conservatives are busy twitching like oil-addicted junkies looking for a fix.

★ Our long-term national security, economic stability, and possible existence as a species depend on solving the problem. That makes global warming a moral issue, a family values issue, and, in the event of severe weather changes, a fashion issue.

STEP 3: REFUTE BOGUS CLAIMS

The "It's-All-Just-a-Big-Liberal-Hoax" Defense

Kick-ass comeback: No credible scientist refutes the overwhelming evidence that global warming is man-made. The only "experts" who claim there's a debate are the pseudoscientists and so-called "biostitutes" funded by the energy companies to say that up is down, black is white, and SUV fumes are your friend. We built an entire foreign policy doctrine of preemption based on responding to even the most remote threats. Shouldn't we apply the same thinking to a threat that's a virtual certainty?

The "We-Can't-Run-the-Risk-of-Crippling-Our-Economy" Defense

Kick-ass comeback: The idea that we have to choose between protecting the economy and protecting the environment is a false choice. We can do both.

Global warming presents an opportunity to tap American ingenuity to create new technologies, new jobs, and new growth industries that can boost our economy. The cost of doing nothing could total trillions annually over the next century, according to various studies. What's the smarter move—to invest in a solution now or go back to watching *Dancing with the Stars* and hope for the best?

The "We've-Got-Bigger-Problems-to-Worry-About" Defense

Kick-ass comeback: Global warming is a national security issue. If we don't establish energy independence, break our addiction to foreign oil, and prevent the kind of planetary chaos that could come with drastic climate change, we will have much more to fear from the effects of global warming than from global terrorism. Think of the Earth as the *Titanic* taking on water, only with fewer lifeboats and without the Celine Dion soundtrack.

STEP 4: BOTTOM-LINE IT

We don't have time to pussyfoot around and pretend the problem doesn't exist. We're facing an imminent threat to our way of life, and we need to put people in power who have a clue. We had a Manhattan Project to build an atomic bomb and an Apollo program to reach the moon. Why not a similar program to find alternative energy sources so we all don't end up breathing through snorkels?

The people who still say that global warming isn't real are actually in the same boat with the Flat Earth Society. They get together and party on Saturday nights with the folks that believe the moon landing was in a movie lot in Arizona.

—Al Gore

The greatest hoax ever perpetrated on the American people.

—Sen. James Inhofe (R-OK), former chairman of the Senate Committee on Environment and Public Works, on global warming

What could be more pertinent to the culture of life than keeping life going on planet Earth?

—Bill Maher

Global Warming, by the Numbers

0: The number of peer-reviewed academic studies on global warming, out of nearly one thousand, that disputed the fact that humans are responsible for global warming

$16 million: The amount of money Exxon paid to advocacy groups to "manufacture uncertainty" about the science behind global warming between 1998 and 2005, according to the Union of Concerned Scientists

10: The number of years before we cross a point of no return, according to leading scientists

166: The number of countries and governmental entities that have signed the Kyoto Protocol on climate change, which the United States has not signed

86: The number of evangelical Christian leaders who broke with other conservatives to back a major initiative to combat global warming

20: The number of feet below sea level the Bush family's boat launch in Kennebunkport will be if either the Antarctic or Greenland ice sheet melts

TAXES AND THE ECONOMY: WHY CONSERVATIVES ARE FISCALLY FOOLHARDY

STEP 1: FRAME YOUR ARGUMENT

Pin blame for the middle-class squeeze and under-performing economy on the fanatical conservative ideologues who sold us reckless, upper-class tax cuts. Tell them that listening to conservatives talk about fiscal discipline is like listening to Bush explain how "reading is the basics for all learning."

STEP 2: MAKE YOUR CASE

- ★ Conservatives had their chance to implement their economic vision, and promptly trapped us all under the weight of crushing debt and an Everest of new government spending.

- ★ We are paying for Bush's orgy of tax favors to the wealthy with money borrowed from China, Japan, and Saudi Arabia, and sticking our kids' generation with the bill (which they will be sure to thank us for when they dump us in that low-rent retirement trailer park).

★ Thanks to ridiculous gas prices, soaring healthcare costs, and stagnant wages brought on by conservative economic policies, the middle class has gotten squeezed like a fat man flying coach in the middle seat.

STEP 3: REFUTE BOGUS CLAIMS

The "Democrats-Will-Raise-Taxes-and-Ruin-the-Economy" Defense

Kick-ass comeback: Democrats believe in cutting taxes for the middle class and restoring the perfectly reasonable tax rates the wealthiest Americans were paying during the Clinton years. Back then, we had the longest economic expansion in history and broad prosperity that created 22 million new jobs. And funny thing—that happened *after* he raised taxes on the rich.

The "Democrats-Just-Want-to-Wage-Class-Warfare" Defense

Kick-ass comeback: If anyone is waging class warfare, it's Republicans. They have shifted the overall tax burden away from the rich, adopted policies that reward wealth over work, and created loopholes enabling the rich to avoid paying their fair share. The average middle class worker, meanwhile, is lucky if he can even get through to tech support in India, where the outsourced American Dream is thriving. Just curious, but if this is a class war, who's side are you on?

The "Republicans-Are-Committed-to-Limited-Government" Defense

Kick-ass comeback: Maybe in the bizarro world, but conservatives' actions prove that promise is nothing more than empty sloganeering. When they had total power, they grew government at a rate not seen since the 1960s while creating such a budgetary disaster that not even FEMA could find a way to make it worse. Should we chalk that up to rank hypocrisy or just bad accounting?

STEP 4: BOTTOM-LINE IT

We learned the hard way about what conservatives' economic priorities truly are: taking money out of Joe Sixpack's wallet to pay for Donald Trump's tax cut. That's not an economic plan.

That's a Ponzi scheme. Been there, done that, still paying the bill.

★ ★ ★ ★ ★ ★ ★ ★ ★ ★ ★ ★ ★

Economic Insanity, by the Numbers

$131 billion: The average annual federal deficit under Republican presidents since 1960

$30 billion: The average annual federal deficit under Democratic presidents since 1960

$44,000: The annual amount Republican tax cuts saved the richest 1 percent, compared to a few hundred dollars for most Americans

430 times: The gap between the income levels of CEOs vs. average workers (ten times more than it was a generation ago)

10: The percentage of Americans who own 80 percent of all stocks

$223 million: The cost of the infamous "Bridge to Nowhere" that Republicans earmarked for an Alaskan town of fifty people

George Bush giving tax cuts is like Jim Jones giving Kool-Aid. It tastes good but it'll kill you.

—Reverend Al Sharpton

The administration says the American people want tax cuts. Well, duh. The American people also want drive-through nickel beer night. The American people want to lose weight by eating ice cream. The American people love the Home Shopping Network because it's commercial-free.

—Comedian Will Durst

You work three jobs? Uniquely American, isn't it? I mean, that is fantastic that you're doing that.

—George W. Bush,
to a divorced mother of three

★ ★ ★ ★ ★ ★ ★ ★

Defending America: Why Conservatives Aren't Up To the Job

STEP 1: FRAME YOUR ARGUMENT

Explain how—contrary to conservatives' claims to being strong on defense—they have made the world a more dangerous place while leaving us vulnerable to attack by everything from flood waters to killer spinach.

STEP 2: MAKE YOUR CASE

★ Thanks to the conservatives running U.S. foreign policy, there are now more terrorists in the world trying to kill us than there were on 9/11 (roughly one hundred terrorists for every clump of brush that Bush has diligently cleared from his ranch).

★ We're not only losing the Iraq war, but Afghanistan has gone to hell too, with both the opium and terrorist trades flourishing once again.

★ The Hurricane Katrina fiasco proved that conservatives have no clue about how to keep Americans safe, while neatly demonstrating what happens when you take the conservative governing philosophy, add water, and shake vigorously.

★ If you're "with us or against us," it's a bad sign when we've turned 95 percent of the Earth's population against us.

STEP 3: REFUTE BOGUS CLAIMS

The "Vote-Republican-or-Die" Defense

Kick-ass comeback: Americans have had it with that kind of fearmongering. They've had it with conservatives who shamelessly invoke 9/11 at every turn, warn of imminent mushroom clouds, and raise terror alert levels when it's politically convenient (like right after the Democratic convention in 2004). Fear is supposed to be the weapon of terrorists. So what does it say when Republicans have nothing to run on but fear itself?

The "Republicans-Are-the-True-Defenders of Freedom" Defense

Kick-ass comeback: While we've supposedly been fighting to promote freedom abroad, Republicans have been trampling our freedoms at home. With little debate, Republicans sanctioned warrantless wiretapping, repealed habeas corpus (part of the rule of law going back *eight hundred years* to the Magna Carta), and gave the president the authority to arrest and indefinitely detain anyone without trial. Would you seriously trust a Democratic president, say, Hillary Clinton, with that kind of power?

The "Republicans-Will-Do-Whatever-It-Takes-to-Defend-America" Defense

Kick-ass comeback: Two words: Hurricane Katrina. If that's "doing whatever it takes," we are all toast. What about attempting to outsource our port security to the highest Arab bidder or whoring ourselves to the Saudi royal family to feed our dependence on foreign oil? Honestly, what do we tell the children?

STEP 4: BOTTOM-LINE IT

We entrusted conservative Republicans with the job of protecting America, and they proved as derelict in their duties as an AWOL National Guard pilot on a drunken bender. If we're going to be serious about defending the homeland, defending our government from conservatives would be a good place to start.

★ ★ ★ ★ ★ ★ ★ ★ ★ ★ ★ ★ ★ ★ ★

Defending America, by the Numbers

100+: The number of meetings the Clinton administration held on the Osama bin Laden threat during the last two years of his presidency

0: The number of meetings the Bush administration held on the bin Laden threat prior to 9/11

1: The rank Homeland Security gave to Indiana in its database listing the most "target-rich" states for terrorist attacks, with 50 percent more potential sites listed than New York and nearly twice as many as California

0: The number of New York City landmarks included in that same database's listing of "national monuments and icons" vulnerable to terrorist attack

1 each: The number of Amish popcorn factories, kangaroo conservation centers, mule parades, and petting zoos Homeland Security listed as vulnerable to attack

75: The percentage of Brits who say Bush poses a danger to world peace, ranking just below bin Laden (87) and above Kim Jong-il (69)—and they're *our closest ally*

One of the hardest parts of my job is to connect Iraq to the war on terror.

—George W. Bush

....

This is the Law and Order and Terror government. It promised protection—or at least amelioration—against all threats: conventional, radiological, or biological. It has just proved that it cannot save its citizens from a biological weapon called standing water.

—MSNBC's Keith Olbermann, on the botched response to Hurricane Katrina

IRAQ: WHY IT'S A "CATASTROFUCK"*

(* Defined by Jon Stewart as when a hellhole meets a cataclysm)

STEP 1: FRAME YOUR ARGUMENT

Explain that Iraq is a deadly distraction from the real war on terror and pin blame not only on Bush but also on all the equally delusional conservatives who cheered the war every step of the way with their rainbow "terror-alert" pom-poms.

STEP 2: MAKE YOUR CASE

★ We lost the war, thanks to the utter incompetence of Bush, Cheney, and the neocons, who used a patchwork of lies to sell us on a faith-based war plan drawn up on the back of a cocktail napkin.

★ The war has made the overall global terrorism threat worse, according to no less than sixteen U.S. intelligence agencies.

★ Our military remains caught in the middle of a civil war trying to play Whack-a-Mole while threats gather elsewhere in the world.

★ The bipartisan Iraq Study Group confirmed we have been left to choose between extremely bad and utterly horrible options, the least bad of which is to pull our troops out and let Iraqis fight it out themselves.

STEP 3: REFUTE BOGUS CLAIMS

The "We Can-Still-Win-the-War" Defense

Kick-ass comeback: Every claim conservatives have ever made about Iraq—from alleged WMDs and Al Qaeda ties to the promise that we'd be "greeted as liberators" and help spread democracy—turned out to be a sham. Now the same geniuses who got us into the mess keep assuring us that victory can be achieved if we just try their new-and-improved strategy. As the saying goes, "Fool me once, shame on you. Fool me twelve times, and you get the next lie free."

The "We-Have-to-Fight-Them-There-So-We-Don't-Fight-Them-Here" Defense

Kick-ass comeback: Our real enemy is Al Qaeda, and Al Qaeda is a bit player at best in Iraq. We're caught in the middle of a civil war raging among Sunnis, Shiites, warlords, foreign terrorists, militias, and exploding freelance anarchists. Al Qaeda, meanwhile, roams free elsewhere in the world. How about we start focusing on the real enemy that attacked us on 9/11? How about we free our military so we can be prepared to respond to actual threats in the future, like, say, Iran or North Korea, who *actually have WMDs?*

Having been attacked by Al Qaeda, for us now to go bombing Iraq in response would be like our invading Mexico after the Japanese attacked us at Pearl Harbor.

—former Bush administration counterterrorism czar Richard Clarke, to Colin Powell, on the day after 9/11, when Bush administration officials began planning to attack Iraq in retaliation

The "Iraq-Will-Explode-into-Chaos-If-We-Cut-and-Run" Defense

Kick-ass comeback: Iraq exploded into chaos about the same time that Bush was prancing around an aircraft carrier with a sock stuffed in his codpiece. Our presence there is doing absolutely no good. The sooner we get out, the fewer soldiers will die, and the less taxpayer dollars we'll squander. It's Vietnam all over again, and we're faced with the same question now as John Kerry posed then: "How do you ask a soldier to be the last man to die for a mistake?"

STEP 4: BOTTOM-LINE IT

The Iraq war has been the worst strategic disaster in U.S. history. That is, until we invade Iran.

★ ★ ★ ★ ★ ★ ★ ★ ★ ★ ★ ★ ★ ★

Iraq, by the Numbers

6,000+: The average annual number of U.S. casualties during the first four years of the Iraq war

655,000: The estimated number of Iraqis who have died since the beginning of the war who wouldn't have died otherwise, according to a 2006 study by American and Iraqi epidemiologists

$8 billion: The amount of money being spent on the Iraq war *per month*

1999: The year in which the U.S. government conducted secret war games that found an invasion of Iraq would likely result in chaos even if the United States were to send in 400,000 troops

0: The number of times Iraq was mentioned in a 2001 State Department report that identified forty-five countries where Al Qaeda was operating

1: The number of times Donald Rumsfeld met with Saddam Hussein

0: The number of times Osama bin Laden met with Saddam Hussein

$20 million: The amount Republicans in Congress set aside in 2006 but never spent to celebrate "V-I Day" for victory in Iraq and Afghanistan

The government that governs best is the government that governs least. And by these standards, we have set up a fabulous government in Iraq.

—Stephen Colbert

....

When they say the terrorists want the Democrats to win, you say, 'Are you insane? George Bush has been a terrorist's wet dream.' He inflames radical hatred against America and then runs on offering to protect us from it. It's like a guy throwing shit on you and then selling you relief from the flies.

—Bill Maher

....

President Bush is going to establish elections there in Iraq. He's going to rebuild the infrastructure. He's going to create jobs. He said if it works there, he'll try it here.

—David Letterman

BUSH: WHY HE'S THE WORST PRESIDENT EVER

STEP 1: FRAME YOUR ARGUMENT

Explain how Bush has been a dangerously incompetent, miserable failure of a president who literally destroyed everything he touched. But don't just blame Bush. Blame conservatism for putting so many nutty ideas in his head and making him such a disastrous "decider."

STEP 2: MAKE YOUR CASE

★ Based on nearly every benchmark he set and promise he made, Bush failed: He said he'd balance the budget (he didn't); he said Saddam had WMDs (he didn't); he said most of his tax cuts would go to the middle class (they didn't); he said he'd be a uniter, not a divider (he got it backwards); and he even said we were going to Mars (and then left us all behind).

STEP 3: REFUTE BOGUS CLAIMS

The "Bush-Went-After-the-Terrorists-and-Made-America-Safer" Defense

Kick-ass comeback: Let's see. He let Osama bin Laden get away in 2001. He got us stuck in a civil war in Iraq that has nothing to do with the global terrorist threat. And there has been more terrorism in the world since 9/11, not less. If that's your definition of safer, what color is the sky in your world?

The "Bush-Created-a-Booming-Economy" Defense

Kick-ass comeback: Other than the richest 1 percent, the only people better off now than they were eight years ago are bankruptcy lawyers, psychotherapists, and political comedians.

George Bush is not Hitler. He would be if he fucking applied himself.

—Margaret Cho

I stand by this man because he stands for things. Not only for things, he stands on things. Things like aircraft carriers, and rubble, and recently flooded city squares. And that sends a strong message that no matter what happens to America she will always rebound with the most powerfully staged photo-ops in the world.

—Stephen Colbert, on Bush

The "Bush-Will-Be-Proven-Right-by-History" Defense

Kick-ass comeback: If by "success" you mean laying the groundwork for World War III, saddling our grandchildren with our debt, packing the courts with right-wing ideologues, ignoring the looming global warming catastrophe, and leaving no female European head of state un-groped, then, yes, "fair and balanced" historians will judge his presidency an unparalleled success.

STEP 4: BOTTOM-LINE IT

Bush's abysmal record is a shining example of what happens when you give a right-wing conservative president unfettered power to implement the conservative vision for America. He had the first Republican governing majority in nearly seventy years, and promptly steered our economy, our military, and America's credibility straight into a ditch. It's exactly what you'd expect from an ideology built around the idea that government doesn't work.

> Herbert Hoover was a shitty president, but even he never conceded an entire metropolis to rising water and snakes. On your watch, we've lost almost all of our allies, the surplus, four airliners, two trade centers, a piece of the Pentagon, and the city of New Orleans. Maybe you're just not lucky. I'm not saying you don't love this country, I'm just wondering how much worse it could be if you were on the other side. So yes, God does speak to you, and what he's saying is, 'Take a hint.'
>
> —Bill Maher, on Bush

★ ★ ★ ★ ★ ★ ★ ★ ★ ★ ★ ★ ★ ★

Bush, by the Numbers

750 and counting: Number of new laws Bush has challenged with signing statements declaring his intent to reinterpret or disregard the laws he just signed

568: The total number of signing statements issued by the previous forty-two presidents combined

$236 billion: The surplus Bush inherited in 2001

$248 billion: The budget deficit in 2006

36 percent: Bush's approval rating at the end of six years in office

66 percent: Bill Clinton's approval rating when he was impeached

2 million: Tax dollars the Republican Congress appropriated to buy Bush a yacht

★ CHAPTER 8 ★

The Conservative Hall of Shame

I have only ever made one prayer to God, a very short one: 'Oh Lord, make my enemies ridiculous.' And God granted it.

—Voltaire

Y ou can add extra bite to your arguments by highlighting outstanding achievements in conservative hypocrisy and idiocy. Happily, there are many fine examples from which to choose.

Here's a rundown of some of the most prominent conservative sex fiends, lunatics, morons, crooks, and chickenhawks who have disgraced national politics in recent years—and earned their place in the Conservative Hall of Shame.

THE WING OF SEX FIENDS, PERVERTS, AND ADULTERERS

ARNOLD SCHWARZENEGGER, THE GROPINATOR

Claim to shame: The legendary sexual exploits of California Governor Arnold Schwarzenegger—from engaging in group sex with other body builders to allegedly groping women on movie sets, during interviews, and at gyms on several continents—inspired cartoonist Garry Trudeau to bestow him with the nickname "Herr Gropenfuhrer."

STROM THURMOND, PUTTING THE "DIX" IN "DIXIECRAT"

Claim to shame: An eight-term senator and one-time presidential candidate, Thurmond was a staunch advocate of segregation, despite having fathered an illegitimate daughter at age twenty-two after a tryst with a sixteen-year-old African American girl working as the family maid (which wasn't revealed until after his death at age one hundred). As Jon Stewart joked, "Thurmond devoted much of his life to the cause of racial segregation, but when it came to separating whites and blacks, he did make an exception for his penis."

BILL O'REILLY, FALAFEL FETISHIST

Claim to shame: The FOX News bloviator settled a sexual harassment lawsuit brought by a former producer who accused him of talking to her in explicit terms about "phone sex, vibrators, threesomes, masturbation, the loss of his virginity, and sexual fantasies." In the most notorious sexual scenario, O'Reilly confused a loofah for a falafel, attempting to seduce his victim by describing lewd acts he hoped to perform on her in the shower using ground chickpeas. Around the same time, he wrote in *The O'Reilly Factor for Kids,* "And guys, if you exploit a girl, it will come back to get you. That's called 'karma.'"

MARK "I'M NEVER TOO BUSY TO SPANK IT" FOLEY

Claim to shame: As cofounder of the congressional caucus on missing and exploited children, ex-congressman Foley was so committed to protecting children from cyber stalkers that he faithfully corresponded with underage male pages to ensure they weren't being exploited. A sampling from one of his instant message exchanges: "How's my favorite young stud doing?...Did you spank it this weekend yourself? . . . Is your little guy limp or growing? . . . What you wearing? . . . Love to slip them off you and grab the one-eyed snake . . . (Page: 'My mom is yelling') . . . Cool, I hope she didn't see anything."

REVEREND TED "SAY NO TO GAY MARRIAGE, SAY YES TO GAY HOOKERS" HAGGARD

Claim to shame: A one-time spiritual adviser to President Bush, Haggard resigned as president of the 30-million-member National Association of Evangelicals amid allegations he had been having methamphetamine-fueled gay sex. The hooker he frequented over a period of three years said he decided to out Haggard because of his hypocritical moralizing and outspoken opposition to gay marriage. "You know you're in trouble when you've ceded the moral high ground to a drug-dealing prostitute," quipped Jon Stewart.

LARRY "WIDE STANCE" CRAIG

Claim to shame: Senator Larry Craig (R-estroom) gave "new meaning to the word caucusing" (David Letterman) when he was caught playing footsie in the men's room with his infamous "wide stance." Craig announced his resignation, then later reversed his decision after "talking it over with guy in stall number 3" (Conan O'Brien), angering his Republican colleagues, some of whom "stopped having sex with him" (Jimmy Kimmel). The staunchly anti-gay lawmaker denied being a hypocrite, saying, "Hey, I wasn't trying to marry the cop in the bathroom" (O'Brien). Later, he was inducted into the Idaho Hall of Fame—not the entire hall, "just the men's room" (Jay Leno).

RUDY GIULIANI, AMERICA'S ADULTERER

Claim to shame: After carrying on an affair while serving as New York mayor, Giuliani announced at a press conference that he was divorcing his second wife—without bothering to tell her first. Because if you're going to leave the mother of your two children, who better to deliver the news delicately than New York tabloid reporters?

THE WING OF UNHINGED LUNATICS AND SOCIOPATHS

REVEREND PAT "FATWA" ROBERTSON

Claim to shame: The good reverend and pillar of Christian love has prayed for the deaths of Supreme Court justices; suggested nuking the State Department; called for the assassination of Venezuela's president; and claims he can leg-press 2,000 pounds, thanks to his delicious "age-defying protein shake," also available for purchase in pancake form.

ANN "COULTERGEIST"

Claim to shame: The right-wing telebimbo has fantasized about forcibly converting Muslims to Christianity; blowing up the *New York Times* building; making torture a televised spectator sport; and putting rat poison in Supreme Court Justice Stevens's crème brulée. Not even 9/11 widows have been spared her wrath, with Coulter saying, "I have never seen people enjoying their husband's death so much."

BILL FRIST, KITTEN KILLER

Claim to shame: Long before the physician-turned-lawmaker was diagnosing vegetative patients from the Senate floor and claiming you can get AIDS from sweat and tears, Frist used to adopt kittens from animal shelters. He treated them as pets for a while, and then—to train himself for a career in healthcare—he killed them as part of medical experiments. Columnist Alexander Cockburn dubbed Frist "the cat world's answer to Dr. Mengele."

BILL O'REILLY, INSURGENT WINDBAG

Claim to shame: As part of his unflinching commitment to provide the straight facts without spin, O'Reilly has sanctioned an Al Qaeda terrorist strike on San Francisco; expressed his wish that Hurricane Katrina had taken out the United Nations; and said one day Al Franken is going to "get a knock on his door and life as he's known it will change forever." David Letterman was being charitable when he told O'Reilly, "I have the feeling about 60 percent of what you say is crap."

REVEREND JERRY "BLOW THEM AWAY IN THE NAME OF THE LORD" FALWELL

Claim to shame: The founder of the "Moral Majority" blamed the 9/11 attacks on the abortionists, feminists, gays, lesbians, the ACLU, and other pagans who made God mad; suggested that Lucifer would make a less objectionable presidential candidate than Hillary Clinton; and demonstrated his keen understanding of scripture when he said we need to hunt down terrorists and "blow them all away in the name of the Lord." Which begs the question: shouldn't we be concerned about our own radical fundamentalist clerics?

The Wing of Morons

Right-wing nut jobs, in their own words . . .

"Our enemies are innovative and resourceful, and so are we. They never stop thinking about new ways to harm our country and our people, and neither do we."

—George W. Bush

"There are neighborhoods in Baghdad where you and I could walk through those neighborhoods today."

—John McCain, prior to visiting a Baghdad market while being flanked by twenty-two soldiers, ten armored Humvees, and two Apache attack helicopters

"I even accept for the sake of argument that sexual orgies eliminate social tensions and ought to be encouraged."

—Supreme Court Justice Antonin Scalia

"We don't all agree on everything. I don't agree with myself on everything."

—Rudy Giuliani

"So many of the people in the arena here, you know, were underprivileged anyway, so this (chuckle)—this is working very well for them."

—Barbara Bush, on Hurricane Katrina evacuees in the Houston Astrodome

"We need to execute people like [John Walker Lindh] in order to physically intimidate liberals."

—Ann Coulter

"Nothing is more important in the face of a war than cutting taxes."

—Tom DeLay

"I am not going to give you a number for it because it's not my business to do intelligent work."

—Donald Rumsfeld, when asked to estimate the number of Iraqi insurgents while testifying before Congress

"The Internet is not something you just dump something on. It's not a big truck. It's a series of tubes."
—Ted Stevens, former chairman of the Senate Commerce Committee

"Too many whites are getting away with drug use... Too many whites are getting away with drug sales... The answer is to go out and find the ones who are getting away with it, convict them, and send them up the river, too."
—Rush Limbaugh, in 1995

"I am addicted to prescription pain medication."
—Limbaugh, in 2003

"I saw this toilet bowl. How many times do you get away with this—to take a woman, grab her upside down, and bury her face in a toilet bowl?"
—Arnold Schwarzenegger, describing a rehearsal for a scene in *Terminator 3*

The Wing of Crooks and Corrupt Weasels

TOM "COCKROACH" DELAY

Claim to shame: The pest exterminator-turned-lawmaker-turned-lawbreaker was forced to resign as House majority leader after being indicted on campaign finance conspiracy charges. Upon leaving Congress, DeLay invoked Martin Luther King, saying, "Free at last, free at last. Thank God Almighty, I'm free at last." As Bill Maher noted, "I think it's great that Tom is so into the black experience, because in prison he's going to be experiencing a lot of it."

JACK "CAN YOU SMELL MONEY?" ABRAMOFF

Claim to shame: A high-powered Republican lobbyist, Abramoff was the central figure in one of the biggest corruption scandals in Washington history. He passed millions in bribes to a top Republican congressman, and before being sentenced to a six-year prison term, the FBI actually set him up with his own desk because he had so much dirt to dish.

DUKE "SUPERSIZE MY BRIBE" CUNNINGHAM

Claim to shame: The former congressman is currently serving eight years in prison after pleading guilty to taking $2.4 million in bribes and shaking down defense contractors while serving on the House Intelligence Committee. He even created his own bribe "menu" listing the government contracts his customers could "order" in exchange for specific cash payments. Cunningham's suitors also allegedly threw rollicking poker and hooker parties for him and his congressional cohorts to buy them off, because if you're going to disgrace your office, why not go all-in?

SCOOTER LIBBY, CHENEY'S CHENEY

Claim to shame: Dick Cheney's former chief of staff was convicted on four felony counts in the investigation into the Bush administration's outing of a CIA operative. He's considered a prime candidate to be pardoned by President Bush before he leaves office because any guy with a name like Scooter who has spent time in prison will, in all likelihood, have already suffered enough.

HONORABLE MENTION

Claude Allen, Bush's former top domestic policy adviser, was forced to resign after being arrested in a refund theft scheme, in which he used fake receipts to "return" some $5,000 worth of merchandise that he did not pay for to Target and other stores.

Chickenhawk, n: A person enthusiastic about war, provided someone else fights it; particularly when that enthusiasm is undimmed by personal experience with war; most emphatically when that lack of experience came in spite of ample opportunity in that person's youth.

—The Chickenhawk Database

THE WING OF CHICKENHAWKS

 Match the following Republican war-mongers with their excuse for weaseling out of the Vietnam War.

1. George W. Bush
2. Dick Cheney
3. Rush Limbaugh
4. Tom DeLay
5. Trent Lott

(a) Busy nursing the cyst on his ass
(b) Claimed minority youths had taken up so many slots that there was no room for patriotic folks like him
(c) Dedicated himself instead to raising school spirit as a college cheerleader
(d) Knocked up his wife to get a deferment; later explained he had "other priorities" during the war
(e) Used his father's connections to get plum spot in National Guard, where he went AWOL

Answers: 1. e, 2. d, 3. a, 4. b, 5. c

Other noteworthy chickenhawks: Bill O'Reilly, Karl Rove, Mitch McConnell, Roy Blunt, Newt Gingrich, Dennis Hastert, Bill Kristol, John Ashcroft, Saxby Chambliss, Paul Wolfowitz, Brit Hume, Roger Ailes, Michael Savage, and the 101st Fighting Keyboardists (right-wing bloggers known for agitating for war in their pajamas).

CHAPTER 9

You've Won the Battle, Now Help Win the War

We gotta take these bastards. Now we could do it with conventional weapons. But that could take years and cost millions of lives. No, I think we have to go all-out. I think that this situation absolutely requires a really futile and stupid gesture be done on somebody's part.

—from *Animal House*

Now that you've succeeded in tearing apart, taunting, or humiliating your opponents, you can set your sights on loftier goals—helping to defeat conservatism at large. There are, of course, the conventional things you should do as a matter of habit: vote, get others to vote, contribute money to campaigns and causes, and get educated (for a list of essential political resources, news sites, and blogs, see FightConservatives.com).

But if you want to make a serious ruckus, you need to step up your game. With that in mind, we offer . . .

Six Unconventional Things You Can Do to Save the World from Conservatives

1. MAKE LIBERAL BABIES

In the long-term effort to win recruits, liberals are facing a fundamental problem: Conservatives are currently outbreeding liberals. According to the 2004 General Social Survey, conservatives are reproducing at a rate that is 41 percent higher than liberals. It's a trend that could spell lasting doom for the liberal cause if liberals don't quickly take matters into their own bedrooms.

What you need: A liberal of opposite gender, mood music.

What you do: We don't really need to spell it out here, but let's just say it's time for liberals to get busy and start popping out new foot soldiers or, if you prefer, adopting them. For those still looking for that special someone, you can do your part to replenish the liberal ranks by going to DemocraticMatch.com or LiberalHearts.com today.

2. STALK A REPUBLICAN CANDIDATE

Sure, you can write your congressman. But if you really what to make an impact, follow him around with a video camera. There's a Republican candidate out there just waiting to self-immolate, and it's your job to provide the match.

What you need: A video camera, a campaign schedule, and a YouTube account.

What you do: By becoming a fixture at public events, you will be in a unique position to record any idiotic utterances that may sink his career. That's what S. R. Sidarth did when he followed around former Republican Senator George Allen (R-Unemployed). When Allen ridiculed the twenty-year-old American of Indian descent by calling him "macaca" (a term for monkeys used as an ethnic slur in certain parts of the world), the video ended up on YouTube and sent Allen's campaign into a tailspin (ultimately tipping control of the Senate to the Democrats). The next party-crashing Democratic hero could be you.

3. STAGE A CLEVER PROTEST

If you really want to advance your political interests while making a name for yourself, you need to do something that will grab headlines.

What you need: A vivid imagination, a sense of irony, a lawyer.

What you do: Pick a topical issue and put your own spin on it. Good real-world examples: camping out in a tree for a few years to protest logging; getting naked with friends and spelling out antiwar messages on a hillside; and attempting to seize Supreme Court Justice David Souter's home and turn it into the "Lost Liberty Hotel" in protest of the court's ruling on eminent domain seizures.

4. EXORCISE CONSERVATIVE MEDIA BIAS

The so-called "liberal media" has been screwing over liberals for years. Yet conservatives are the ones who gripe incessantly about bias. They release the hounds at a moment's notice and flood news organizations and their corporate suites with phone calls, emails, and letters. As a result, many cowed political journalists bend over backward to prattle off Republican talking points, for fear of being branded as "liberals." And that's how liberals—and the truth—get violated.

What you need: TV, radio, Internet access, and an axe to grind.

What you do: Forget letters to the editor. Write directly to the reporter or to his or her editor or producer to complain about a biased story. That's how you can get inside their heads. In more egregious cases—say, if ABC is running a hit piece disguised as a documentary blaming 9/11 on Clinton—make noise at the corporate level, boycott advertisers, or write investor relations and tell them you're selling off your shares (even if you don't own any). Your goal is to be every bit as big a pain in the ass as conservatives are.

5. BITCH-SLAP CONSERVATIVES WITH YOUR WALLET

Corporations may have our political system by the balls, but that doesn't mean you can't do anything about it. By patronizing companies that primarily support liberal causes and candidates and shunning those that back conservative ones, you can kick them where it hurts most: their profit margins.

What you need: Info from BuyBlue.org or Opensecrets.org, plus disposable income.

What you do: Support your local businesses or patronize Democratic-friendly corporations like Costco; Barnes & Noble; Bed, Bath & Beyond; Google; Hyatt; or Starbucks. Avoid Exxon, Pfizer, General Motors, Marriott, Outback Steakhouse, or other companies whose political action committees or top executives are reliable contributors to the GOP. You can do the same with your investments, putting your money into progressive-oriented or socially responsible mutual funds, instead of typical investments that feed the conservative corporate beasts.

6. HAUNT REPUBLICANS FROM THE GRAVE

If you can figure out a way to vote while dead, as many decomposing Chicagoans have over the years, great. But if you want to make a truly memorable political statement, try your obituary.

What you need: To be dead.

What you do: Ask your loved ones to honor your memory the way the family of Grant Urry of Massachusetts did ("Friends are asked to remember him by voting Democratic"), or the way the family of Theodore Roosevelt Heller of Illinois did ("In lieu of flowers, please send acerbic letters to Republicans").

After-*Words*

If you can't answer a man's argument, all is not lost; you can still call him vile names.

—Elbert Hubbard

WHEN ALL ELSE FAILS: 27,000 WAYS TO INSULT CONSERVATIVES

Can't persuade anyone to your way of thinking? Kill 'em with words instead. The following handy chart contains 27,000 potential insults that you can lob at conservatives. Choose a word from each column, string them together, and fire away at all the "unmedicated, sex-obsessing hypocrites" or "lying, reality-denying Repugnicans" in your midst.

Column A	Column B	Column C
unhinged	Bible-thumping	wingnuts
unmedicated	warmongering	extremists
brainless	gas-guzzling	blowhards
slack-jawed	gun-toting	rednecks
inbred	knuckle-dragging	hypocrites
lying	Constitution-shredding	McCarthyites
bedwetting	FOX News-humping	fascists
sanctimonious	privacy-invading	demagogues
puritanical	hooker-patronizing	theocrats
confused	male page-seducing	revisionists
delusional	race card-playing	bigots
incompetent	deficit-expanding	zealots
authoritarian	Big Brother-worshipping	prudes
un-American	truthiness-telling	douche bags
intolerant	dissent-stifling	bullies
greedy	civil liberty-seizing	sociopaths
Orwellian	propaganda-dispensing	bloviators
deranged	torture-sanctioning	troglodytes
apocalyptic	hate-spewing	morons
fanatical	dictatorship-endorsing	Busheviks
selfish	Armageddon-yearning	Repugnicans
bloodthirsty	fearmongering	chickenhawks
clueless	Clinton-blaming	wackjobs
shameless	sex-obsessing	homophobes

Column A	Column B	Column C
heartless	election-stealing	totalitarians
arrogant	religion-perverting	Neanderthals
obnoxious	girlie-men-taunting	trailer trash
corrupt	crony-caressing	elitists
militant	NRA-genuflecting	xenophobes
ignorant	reality-denying	phonies

Acknowledgments

This book would not have been necessary if it hadn't been for the politicians on both sides who have worked so diligently to divide the country. Nor would it have been possible—or at least not as much fun to write—without the inspiration provided by Jon Stewart, Stephen Colbert, Bill Maher, Dennis Miller, and political humorists everywhere who put politics in perspective and help dull the pain.

I am indebted to my editor, Deb Werksman; her assistant, Susie Benton; and to the staff at Sourcebooks, whose hard work and enthusiasm made this book a reality, and to my agent, Barret Neville, whose editorial guidance and vision helped shape this project.

Many thanks to Thomas Fahy, who offered indispensable feedback, careful editing, and unflagging support from the beginning, and to Todd Smithline, Lou Kipilman, Joshua Swartz, Lee Levine, Max Zarzana, Josh Archibald, Daniel Wasson, and Sarah Schroeder—all of whom provided valuable assistance and shrewd insights (as well as a few good punch lines) during many stages of the writing process. I'd also like to give a special shout-out to John Thong Nein for challenging me to a war of wits (the shoe is now on the other foot).

My family provided not only inspiration but, somewhat inadvertently, much of the field research that helped inform this book. I am grateful for the love and support of my parents, Ken and Caryl, who taught me the value of tolerance and spirited debate, and my brother, Todd, who taught me the importance of defending my position, especially while being hunted with a BB gun. To the DeCastros, a special salute to Mike for embracing his designation as "Uncle Blowhard" with a passion, Lois for her creative inspiration, and Baylee for living the radical liberal dream. To Jessica Garrett, Patty, Neil, and the entire Smithline clan, thank you for your loving encouragement and the lively conversations, and for demonstrating the importance of communicating in crisp sound bites.

I am also endlessly grateful to many friends for their unfailing support: David Ziring, Alison Hickey, Shannon Farley, Danielle Svetcov, Alex

Kazan, Aviva Rosenthal, Liana Schwarz, Jodi and Andy Brown, Lesley Reidy, Kim O'Farrell, Marty Chester, Dave Uram, Mitch Cox, Rebecca Bagdadi, Jeremy and Melody Hannebrink-Vance, Carol Brydolf, the Suffin family, and the numerous other family members and friends who took time to share their political wisdom and partisan horror stories.

I'd also like to acknowledge several important influences that shaped my political and humor sensibilities: Matt Dorf, my former bureau chief, who schooled me in the ways of Washington; Donal Brown, my high school journalism teacher, who showed me how to kill 'em with words; Dave Kreines, a master of both words and wit, and one of the best friends I ever knew; and the late Duane Garrett, one of the funniest commentators and most brilliant political minds of his generation.

And most importantly, I am grateful beyond words to my wife, Laura, who inspires me every day. Her abiding faith, brilliant insights, and sharp editing helped make every part of this book better. Her love and laughter make every part of life better, too.

About the Author

Daniel Kurtzman chronicles the absurdities of politics as editor of politicalhumor.about.com, the popular website that is part of The New York Times Company's About.com network. As a former Washington correspondent-turned-political satirist, his work has appeared in the *San Francisco Chronicle*, Salon.com, JTA, and the *Funny Times*, among other publications. He lives with his wife, Laura, in the San Francisco Bay Area, where he enjoys engaging in political squabbles with "red" and "blue" people alike. As an equal opportunity offender, Kurtzman is also the author of *How to Win a Fight with a Liberal*.

www.FightConservatives.com